FOREWORD

When asked to write these few introductory words I hardly expected to find myself writing the foreword to what is undoubtedly now the most popular mass-battle fantasy game on the market! What I was expecting was to be able to say that Kings of War has come of age with this, its second edition, always something of a milestone in the history of a game. I would have – and can still – acknowledge that the original Kings of War game has gained a loyal and growing following amongst fantasy wargamers. Many converts have found themselves won over by a mixture of solid game play, straight-forward but elegant mechanics, and an approach to development that plainly puts the player first. This new edition represents another stride in the same direction, and is sure to appeal both to existing devotees and to those discovering the game for the first time.

So well done Mantic – and well done especially to its creator and designer Alessio Cavatore. I have worked together with Alessio on many gaming projects over the years, both historical and fantasy, and have always appreciated his clear and focussed approach to game design, instinct for uncluttered rules, and – most of all – boundless and unquenchable enthusiasm for games and gaming. I think I can confidently say that you'll find plenty of those qualities in Kings of War along with the surety and experience that always comes with a second edition. So, enough from me, muster the ranks for battle and ready the beasts, let arrows fly and dice roll, for now is the time for Kings of War.

Rick Priestley

INTRODUCTION

Welcome to Kings of War!

Kings of War is a mass-battle fantasy wargame set in the world of Mantica, taking all of the fantasy archetypes and embedding them into a rich history full of exciting characters and enigmatic new races. This book contains all of the core rules for the game, along with complete army lists for eleven different forces, and a selection of magical artefacts for them to carry into battle.

This latest edition brings together everything that we've learnt in the last six years, after a very popular first edition, two Kickstarters, an ever-growing miniatures range, and thousands of games. The loyal fans who have been with us through the previous editions will be able to see the progress that has been made. We simply couldn't have done this without our wonderful community – the copious amounts of feedback and many long hours of hard work from our volunteer Rules Committee have made this the most solid set of rules we've ever put out – we couldn't be prouder. Huge thanks to every one of you.

On our website, you'll find free introductory rules and army lists so that you can introduce your friends and club members to the new and exciting world of the Kings of War game. On our forums, you can leave your opinions, ideas and feedback. Please keep it coming!

www.manticgames.com/Forum.html

Devastation and slaughter await...

CONTENTS

CREDITS

Game Design
Alessio Cavatore

Kings of War Rules Committee
Matt Gilbert, Daniel King, Sami Mahmoud,
Chris Morris, Mark Smith, Nick Williams

Background
Michael Grey, Guy Haley, Mark Latham,
Thomas Pike, Anthony Reynolds, Greg D Smith

Sculpting
Gregor Adrian, Juan Miguel López Barea,
Ben Calvert-Lee, Russ Charles, Gregory
Clavilier, Derek Miller, Gary Morley, Bob
Naismith, Dave Neild, Nicolas Nguyen, Juan
Navarro Perez, Tim Prow, Sylvain Quirion,
Steve Saunders, Ben Skinner, Luigi Terzi,
Remy Tremblay, James van Schaik, Kevin White

Painting
Luke Barker, Mark Bedwell, Andrew Chesney,
Conflict in Colour, Matt Gilbert, Golem
Painting Studio, Dave Neild, Paul Scott
Miniatures, Chris Straw, Chris Webb, Andrew
Wedmore, Nick Williams, Winterdyne
Commission Modelling

Art
Robin Carey, Shen Fei, Roberto Cirillo,
Heath Foley, Des Hanley, Yann Hoarau,
Ralph Horsley, Stef Kopinski, Alan Lathwell,
Phil Moss, Michael Rechlin, Jonas Springborg,
Luigi Terzi

Graphic Design
Pete Borlace, Kev Brett, Karen Miksza,
Dylan Owen, Sean Turtle, Chris Webb

Photography
Warwick Kinrade, Mike McVey, Ben Sandum,
Adam Shaw

Playtesters
Sam Rounsevell, Jason Flint, Jason Moorman,
Jez Gurney, Chris "Baz" Beeson, John Beeson,
N. Carpenter, Adam Storey, Bartjan van Kolck,
Asbjørn-Heike Hagen, Andrew Massoura,
HeroicTheNerd

Special Thanks
Warlord Games, Fireforge Games, Gripping
Beast, Artisan Designs and Conquest
Miniatures.

All scenery from owner's collection.

Mantic Games, 193 Hempshill Lane, Bulwell, Nottingham, NG6 8PF, UK

www.manticgames.com

THE RULES

UNITS

In *Kings of War*, all units are made up of one or more models. The number of models that make up a unit is specified in each unit's stats (explained on page 51), and will normally correspond to the number of models you get in boxes supplied by Mantic. These models must be glued onto bases and formed up into units as described below. Each unit belongs to one of the following Types.

Infantry (Inf)

Infantry units come in four sizes:

* Troops consisting of 10 models, arranged five models wide in two ranks.

* Regiments consisting of 20 models, arranged five models wide in four ranks.

* Hordes consisting of 40 models, arranged ten models wide in four ranks.

* Legions consisting of 60 models, arranged ten models wide in six ranks.

Cavalry (Cav)

Cavalry units come in three sizes;

* Troops consisting of 5 models, arranged in a single rank of five.

* Regiments consisting of 10 models, arranged five models wide in two ranks.

* Hordes consisting of 20 models, arranged ten models wide in two ranks.

Large Infantry (Lrg Inf) & Large Cavalry (Lrg Cav)

Large Infantry and Large Cavalry units come in three sizes:

* Regiments consisting of 3 models, arranged in a single rank of three.

* Hordes consisting of 6 models, arranged in two ranks of three models.

* Legions consisting of 12 models, arranged in two ranks of six models.

War Engines (War Eng)

A War Engine is a unit consisting of a single war machine, like a catapult or a bolt thrower. It may also have number of crew models, but these are purely decorative and should be arranged around the machine in a suitably entertaining fashion.

Since the crew is merely decorative, they are ignored for all in-game purposes, such as checking ranges, movement etc.

Monsters (Mon)

A Monster is a unit consisting of a single model – a large and powerful mythical beast or magical construct.

Heroes (Hero/xxx)

A Hero is a unit consisting of a single model. It can be an officer, a sorcerer or even a mighty lord of its race. Heroes vary in size between different races, and can ride many types of mount or even monstrous war-beast, so Heroes always have a tag in bracket specifying what type of unit they belong to – which helps with determining their height and other special rules that are related with certain units.

So a Hero could be a (Hero/Inf), or a (Hero/Cav), or a (Hero/Mon), or a (Hero/Lrg Inf), or a (Hero/Lrg Cav), and though we have not yet conceived a (Hero/War Eng), one never knows...

Sometimes Heroes have options that allow them to choose different mounts – if a mount is chosen, the Hero's unit type will of course change to that of the relative mount, as specified in the Hero's entry.

Base Sizes

Infantry models are based on 20mm square bases, apart from some that will be marked as exceptions in their entry (such as Orcs, which are on 25mm square bases).

Large Infantry models are based on 40mm square bases, apart from some that will be marked as exceptions in their entry (such as Lesser Obsidian Golems, which are on 50mm square bases).

Cavalry models are based on 25x50mm.

Large Cavalry models are based on 50mm square bases, apart from some that will be marked as exceptions in their entry (such as Chariots, which are on 50x100mm).

Monsters and War Engine models are based on 50mm square bases.

Heroes fit on the relevant base of their type unless specified otherwise. For example, a Hero (Inf) will be on a 20mm square base (except for Orc Heroes, which are on 25mm square bases), a Hero (Cav) will be on a 25x50mm base, etc.

Exceptional Base Sizes

You may need a wider or deeper base for exceptionally large heroes, monsters or war engines – in such rare cases, use the smallest base that you can fit your model on.

FRONT, REAR, FLANK

Normally in *Kings of War*, units have four facings: front, rear, left flank and right flank. Each of these facings possesses an 'arc', an area determined by drawing imaginary lines at 45 degree angles from each corner of the unit, as shown in Diagram A.

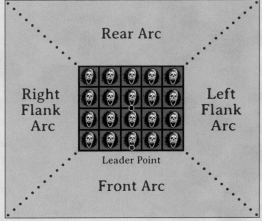

Diagram A – Front, Rear, Flank

UNIT LEADER POINT

The unit leader point is the exact centre of the front edge of a unit's base. The reason why we call it 'leader point' is that some players like to place a suitably imposing model in the centre of the first rank to 'lead' the unit.

Whenever the rules say to take something 'from the unit leader point' (or just 'from the unit leader'), such as a measurement or line of sight, it is from this point in the exact centre of the unit's front edge.

Common Unit Base Sizes

Unit Type	Base Size	Troop	Regiment	Horde	Legion
Infantry	20x20mm	100x40mm	100x80mm	200x80mm	200x120mm
Infantry	25x25mm	125x50mm	125x100mm	250x100mm	250x150mm
Cavalry	25x50mm	125x50mm	125x100mm	250x100mm	n/a
Large Infantry	40x40mm	n/a	120x40mm	120x80mm	240x80mm
Large Cavalry	50x50mm	n/a	150x50mm	150x100mm	300x100mm
Large Cavalry	50x100mm	n/a	150x100mm	150x200mm	300x200mm

CAN THEY SEE?

During the game, you will at times need to determine whether one of your units can see another one, normally an enemy unit that your unit intends to charge or shoot.

Arc of Sight

First, we'll assume that your unit can only see things that are at least partially in its front arc – its 'arc of sight'. The flank and rear arcs are completely blind.

Line of Sight (LOS)

Of course, terrain and other units can still get in the way and hide targets that are in your unit's arc of sight. To determine whether your unit can actually see a target that is in its arc of sight, follow the rules below.

Unit Height

Each unit has a height assigned according to its type:

Unit Type	Height
Infantry	1
Large Infantry	2
Cavalry	2
Large Cavalry	3
Monsters	4
War Engines	1

A hero's height is equal to that of its type. For example, a Hero (Inf) will have a height of 1, while a Hero (Cav) will have a height of 2.

Some units may be an exception and have a different height – this will be specified in their entry (e.g. Orclings are height 0).

Drawing LOS

To determine line of sight, draw an imaginary straight line from the unit leader point to any point of its target's base. If this imaginary line passes over no other unit's base or terrain features, then line of sight is not blocked.

If either your unit or the target unit are taller than any other units or terrain in the way, then line of sight is not blocked. If any units or terrain in the way are the same height or taller than both your unit and the target unit, then line of sight is blocked.

Note that the line of sight does not have to be the shortest line between your unit leader point and the target unit's base; any line from your unit leader point to any part of the target unit's base will do fine.

If you're unsure whether your unit can see a target unit or not, roll a die. On a 4+ it can see it, on 3 or less it cannot.

Terrain and LOS

This is discussed in more detail on page 59.

MEASURING DISTANCES

You can measure any distance at any time you like. Unless otherwise specified, the distance between two units is the distance between the two nearest points of the units' bases.

Keep Your Distance!

In order to avoid confusion, keep your units at least 1" away from enemy units at all times, except when charging or regrouping as explained later. To remove any confusion, ensure that your units are not in base contact with other friendly units at all times.

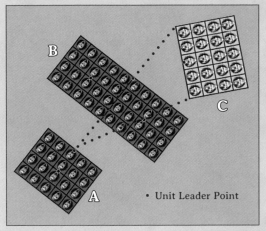

Diagram B1

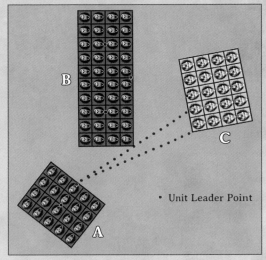

• Unit Leader Point

Diagram B2

Drawing Line of Sight – Example A

Unit A is trying to draw line of sight to Unit C (see Diagram B1). The dotted line represents the line of sight trying to be drawn. If either Unit A or Unit C are taller than Unit B then line of sight is NOT blocked. If Unit B is the same height or taller than both Unit A and Unit C then line of sight is blocked.

Drawing Line of Sight – Example B

In this example (see Diagram B2), Unit B is considered to be as tall as Units A and C and therefore blocks line of sight. Unit A can still see Unit C by looking around the edge of Unit B.

STATS

Each unit in *Kings of War* has a name and a series of statistics (for short, we call them 'stats'), which define how powerful it is in the game. These are:

- **Type.** Whether the unit is Infantry, Cavalry, etc.

- **Unit Size.** How many models the unit comprises of.

- **Speed (Sp).** How fast the unit moves, in inches.

- **Melee (Me).** The score needed by the unit to hit in melee.

- **Ranged (Ra).** The score needed by the unit to hit with ranged attacks. If it has no normal ranged attacks, this is a '–'.

- **Defence (De).** The score the enemy requires to damage the unit.

- **Attacks (Att).** The number of dice the unit rolls when attacking, both at range and in melee.

- **Nerve (Ne).** A combination of the unit's size and its training and discipline, this stat shows how resistant it is to damage suffered.

- **Points (Pts).** How valuable the unit is. Used for picking a force and often for working out victory points, depending on the scenario used.

- **Special.** Any special equipment (like ranged weapons) and rules the unit has.

Example:

Kindred Archers — Infantry

Unit Size	Sp	Me	Ra	De	Att	Ne	Pts
Troop (10)	6	5+	4+	4+	8	10/12	115
Regiment (20)	6	5+	4+	4+	10	14/16	150
Horde (40)	6	5+	4+	4+	20	21/23	250

Special: *Bows*

THE TURN

Much like chess, *Kings of War* is played in turns. Just roll a die to decide who is going to have the first turn – the player winning the die roll decides who goes first. That player moves, shoots and strikes blows in close combat with their units – this concludes Turn 1 of the game. After that, the opposing player takes a turn – Turn 2 of the game, and then the players keep alternating this way until an agreed time limit or turn limit is reached.

A player goes through the following three phases in their turn:

1) Move phase;
2) Shoot phase;
3) Melee phase.

We'll examine each of these phases in detail on the following pages.

Dice

In these rules, whenever we refer to a die or dice, we mean a normal six-sided die, which we call D6. Sometimes we also use terms like 'D3', which is the result of a D6 divided by 2 (rounding up), or 'D6+1', meaning rolling a D6 and adding 1 to the result, or 2D6, which is rolling two dice and adding them together.

Re-Rolls

When you are allowed a re-roll, simply pick up the number of dice you are allowed to re-roll and roll them again. The second result stands, even if it's worse than the first. Regardless of the number of special rules that apply to a particular circumstance, you can never re-roll a re-roll, the second roll always stands.

MOVE

During the Move phase of your turn, pick each of your units in turn and give them one of the following orders:

Halt!
The unit does not move at all.

Change Facing!
The unit remains stationary and can pivot around its centre to face any direction. See Diagram C.

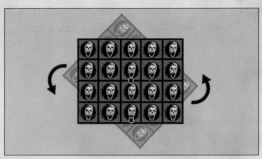

Diagram C – Change Facing

Advance!
The unit can advance straight forward up to a number of inches equal to its Speed. At any point during this move (i.e. before or after advancing, or anywhere along its advance), the unit can also make a single pivot around its centre of up to 90 degrees from its original facing. See Diagram D.

Back!
The unit can move straight backwards at up to half of its Speed. See Diagram E.

Sidestep!
The unit can move sideways straight to its left or straight to its right at up to half of its Speed. See Diagram E.

At the Double!
The unit can advance straight forward up to double its Speed. See Diagram E.

Charge!
This is by far the most exciting of orders. It is also the most complicated and so it's described in detail below.

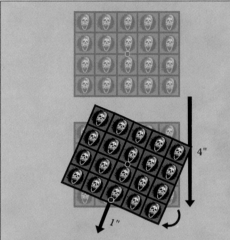

This Skeleton regiment has a Speed of 5" and it's ordered to Advance! first, it's moved 4" straight forward, then it's pivoted around its centre, and finally it completes its advance by moving a futher 1" straight forward.

Diagram D – Advance!

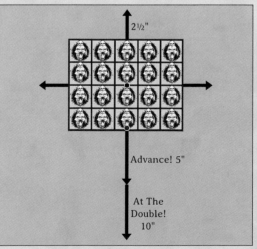

2½"

Advance! 5"

At The Double! 10"

Diagram E – Move

Unit Interpenetration

Interpenetration When Moving

The following rules regulate inter-penetration when a units moves directly forward, backwards or sideways.

Friends

Friendly units can be moved through (except when charging, see below), but you cannot end a unit's move on top of another unit, so you'll have to be sure that your units have enough movement to end up clear of their friends.

Also, at the end of their move, your units must not be in base contact friendly units. This ensures that both you and your opponent can clearly tell them apart.

Enemies

Enemy units, on the other hand, block movement. Your units can never approach to within 1" of them, except when charging or during a pivot.

Interpenetration When Pivoting

In reality, regimented units are more flexible in rearranging their ranks and files than our miniatures, so when a unit is pivoting around its centre it can pivot through both friends and enemy units, and all types of terrain, including blocking terrain and the edge of the table. They must of course still end their pivot (and their entire move) clear of blocking terrain (and completely on the table!), not in base contact with friendly units, and 1" away from enemy units.

Charge!

A charge is the only way your units can move into contact with the enemy. A unit can charge a single enemy unit ('the target') as long as the following conditions are met:

- the target is at least partially in your unit's front arc;

- the unit can see the target;

- the distance between your unit's Leader point and the closest point of the target unit's base is equal to or less than double your unit's Speed;

- there is enough space for your unit to physically move into contact with the target by moving as described below.

Moving Chargers

As they move, charging units can move forward without measuring how much distance they actually cover, and pivot once around their centre up to 90°, at any point during their move.

They must, however, always use the shortest way possible, going around any blocking terrain and any unit in their way (friends and foes). Note that they must go through any area of difficult terrain or obstacle that would normally slow down their movement. These elements of terrain do not slow down Charge moves, but they cause the charging unit to suffer a slight penalty in the ensuing melee.

Once the charging unit is in contact with the target, align it with the side of the target you are charging so that it is flush with it.

Finally, shuffle the chargers sideways until their unit leader point is facing directly opposite the centre of the target unit, or as close as possible to it.

Basically, the main thing that matters during a Charge move is that the unit has physically enough space to move into contact with the target. Note that the unit needs to be able to have at least some of its front physically into contact with the unit being charged, contacting a unit exclusively with the point in the exact corner of the unit is not allowed.

Flank and Rear Charges

If the leader point of the charging unit is in the target's front arc when the order to Charge is given, the unit must charge the target's front facing.

If the leader point of the charging unit is in the target's right or left flank arc when the order to Charge is given, the unit **must** charge the target's appropriate flank facing.

If the leader point of the charging unit is in the target's rear arc when the order to Charge is given, the unit **must** charge the target's rear facing. See Diagram F.

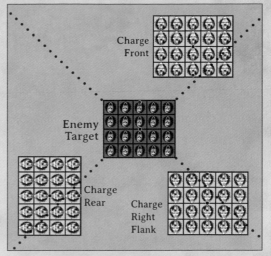

Diagram F – Flank and Rear Charges

Proximity to Enemies

Remember that when charging, units don't have to stay 1" away from enemies, and this means that sometimes a charging unit may end up in contact with both its target and one or more enemy units it has not charged (e.g. when charging a unit that is part of a tight enemy battle line). In this case, you'll have to nudge these enemy units away by an inch or as much as possible to ensure that they are no longer touching.

This represents the charging unit concentrating its fighting efforts against a single enemy, while holding at bay the other enemy units nearby. It might look a bit strange at first, but remember that the enemy units will normally get to charge back into the fight to help their friends in their following turn.

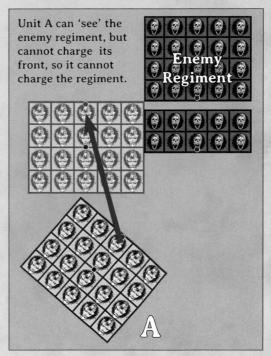

Unit A can 'see' the enemy regiment, but cannot charge its front, so it cannot charge the regiment.

Enemy Regiment

Diagram G – Charging

Corner-to-Corner Charges

In some rare cases, the only possible way for a charger to make physical contact with a target would be by literally having one corner of its frontage in contact with one corner of the target.

These extreme cases are called 'corner to corner' contact – one example of this is shown in Diagram G.

We deem that this is not enough to warrant a sensible charge and combat, so we disallow these charges.

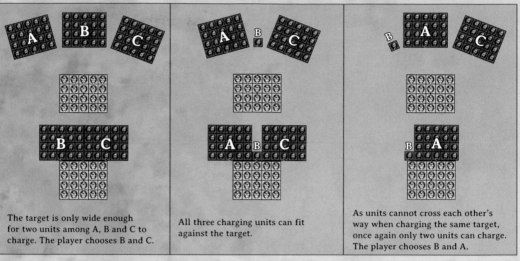

The target is only wide enough for two units among A, B and C to charge. The player chooses B and C.

All three charging units can fit against the target.

As units cannot cross each other's way when charging the same target, once again only two units can charge. The player chooses B and A.

Diagram H – Multiple Charges

Multiple Charges Against the Same Target

If two or more of your units are able to charge the same enemy unit, they can do so, as long as they can fit. Just issue a simultaneous order to all of the units that are charging the same target.

Any units that have charged the same facing of the target will have to share the space available as equally as possible, as long as they can fit after all chargers have moved.

If there isn't enough space for all of the units to fit against the facing of the target they are charging, some of the units will not charge and must be given a different order.

You will notice how it is impossible for three units of exactly the same frontage (e.g. 100mm) to charge the facing of an enemy that has the same width (100mm). This is because corner-to-corner charges are not allowed – so only two such units can charge the same facing, the third will have to be given a different order.

Also note that, in multiple charges, charging units cannot cross each other's way in (see the last example of Diagram H).

Counter Charge

If a unit was charged by one or more enemy units in the previous turn, it may elect to perform a Counter-Charge instead of a regular Charge.

If a unit decides to Counter-Charge then it may only do so against an enemy unit which charged it in the previous turn. It does not need Line of Sight and the enemy unit does not need to be in the front arc, so it may Counter-Charge against units in its flank or rear arcs.

Rather than making a normal Charge move, the unit simply pivots to face the target unit then moves forward until it makes contact with the target's front face. The unit cannot move through friendly or enemy units while making this move, though it may pivot through other units as long as it ends clear of them. Once it makes contact, it aligns with the target unit as normal.

Also note that Counter-Charging to the flank or rear can sometime prove slightly tricky in narrow confines. It is perfectly fine to slide the unit sideways to fit against the front of the enemy, as long as the final position does not overlap any other unit. If the unit cannot fit against the target, then it cannot counter-charge that unit.

All rules that apply in a Charge also apply in a Counter-Charge, unless otherwise specified.

TERRAIN

Elements of terrain make your table look more impressive, but they also make the game more complex, so don't use too much terrain in your first games of *Kings of War*. In war games, terrain is normally made in either of two ways: single terrain pieces or areas of terrain. The rules for both are below. Before the game, it's always a good idea to agree with your opponent how you are going to treat each of the pieces of terrain on the table.

TERRAIN AND MOVEMENT

Terrain Types

There are four types of terrain in *Kings of War:*

- **Blocking Terrain**
  Units cannot move across blocking terrain and must go around it. We recommend treating buildings, high walls and other large pieces as blocking terrain. The edge of the table is also normally treated as blocking terrain. Units can pivot through Blocking Terrain in the same way as other units (see Interpenetration when pivoting on page 55).

- **Difficult Terrain**
  This type of terrain consists of things like woods, crop fields, areas of rocky terrain or scree and so on. They are normally made by gluing a number of pieces of terrain onto a large base. This conveniently shows the area of the terrain – the entire area of this base counts as difficult terrain. While moving At The Double, units treat Difficult Terrain as Blocking Terrain instead.

- **Obstacles**
  Obstacles are long and narrow pieces of terrain, like a low wall, a fence, a hedge, etc. – something that a roughly man-sized creature could see over and clamber across easily. Units can move over obstacles normally (even ending their move on top of them), but cannot cross them while moving 'At the Double'. Obstacles should be no more than 1" high – any higher and they will be Blocking Terrain instead.

- **Decorative Terrain**
  Small pieces of decorative terrain, such as lone trees or bushes, are treated as decorative terrain and are ignored for all in-game purposes. Units can move over/through them freely and can even end their move on top. It's best that decorative terrain like this is removable, but a unit's position can be marked some other way if it can't physically balance on top.

TERRAIN AND LINE OF SIGHT

Terrain Height

Heights of all terrain features should be agreed before the game. As a rough guideline, a piece of terrain has one level of height for each inch of actual physical height, so a 2" high wall would be height 2 for example. See below for some example pieces of terrain and their designations.

Obstacles are height 1 for determining cover, but never block Line of Sight.

Drawing Line of Sight

When working out Line of Sight, terrain blocks LOS to any units behind in the same way as a unit of the same height. For example, a height 2 or higher wall will block LOS between two height 2 units.

Some pieces of terrain, such as rivers and ponds, will be completely flat and never block Line of Sight. As always, these should be agreed with your opponent before the game.

Difficult Terrain

If any part of a unit is inside a piece of difficult terrain then that piece of terrain will not block LOS. In order words, areas of difficult terrain block LOS to units behind them (depending on height, of course), but not to units inside them.

Hills

While standing on a hill, a unit adds that hills height to its own. For example, a height 1 war engine on a height 2 hill would be height 3, while large infantry (height 2) would be height 4 while stood on the hill.

A unit must have the majority of its base on a hill in order to be standing on it.

SHOOT

When you're done moving all of your units, it's time to shoot with any of them that can do so. Pick one of your units at a time, choose a target for them, and let loose!

If you start the Shoot phase and have not issued orders to all of your units, it is assumed that all units you have not ordered during the Move phase have been ordered to Halt.

If a unit has two or more types of ranged attacks (including spells), it can only use one per turn.

MOVING AND SHOOTING

Units that have received an 'At the Double' order that turn are too busy moving to be able to use ranged attacks.

MELEE AND SHOOTING

Units that are in base contact with enemies cannot use or be targeted by ranged attacks, unless specifically allowed.

RANGES

The ranges of the most common weapons used in *Kings of War* are:

- Long rifles, heavy crossbows: 36"

- Bows, crossbows, rifles: 24"

- Harpoon guns, carbines, firebolts (i.e. the flaming attacks used by some supernatural creatures): 18"

- Pistols, javelins, thrown weapons: 12"

If a unit has a ranged attack with a range that is different from the ones above, it will be specified in its special rules.

SHOOTING AND HITTING THE TARGET

Once the target has been picked, roll a number of dice equal to the firing unit's Attacks value. Your unit's dice rolls, with any modifiers that apply, must score a number equal to or higher than its Ranged Attack value in order to hit its target. Discard any dice that score less than that.

Modifiers

A number of factors can affect the chance of hitting a target:

- **–1 Moving.** The firing unit received any order other than Halt that turn. This modifier does not apply to pistols, javelins, thrown weapons.

- **-1 Cover.** The target is in cover (see overleaf).

For each of these factors, deduct one from the score rolled by the dice. For example, if your unit normally needs a 4 or more to hit, but it has moved, you will need 5 or more to hit instead. If the target was in cover as well, you would need 6s.

Picking a Target

A unit can pick a single enemy unit as a target for its ranged attacks as long as the following conditions are met:

- the target is at least partially in the unit's arc of sight.

- the unit has line of sight to the target.

- the distance between the unit leader point and its target is equal to or less than your unit's weapon range.

COVER

In cases when the target unit is partially visible behind a unit or terrain piece, the firing unit might suffer from the negative 'cover' modifier on its rolls to hit. To decide whether the target unit is in cover, draw LOS from the unit leader point of the firing unit to the side of the target unit that the firing unit is in (front, rear, or either flank).

A firing unit ignores any piece of terrain that it is currently within, or in base contact with, for determining whether an enemy unit is in cover, unless the enemy unit is also touching or within the same piece of terrain.

A unit which is standing on a hill ignores any intervening units or pieces of terrain that have an equal or smaller height than the hill when determining if a target is in cover, except for pieces of difficult terrain that the target is within.

The target unit will be in cover if:

• At least half of its base is within difficult terrain, or...

• LOS to at least half of the target facing is blocked, or passes over intervening units or terrain that have a smaller height than the firing or target unit.

Big Targets
Intervening units/terrain that are three height levels smaller than the target offer no cover. For example, height 1 units/terrain do not offer cover to height 4 units.

Not Sure?
In the rare, marginal cases when you're not sure whether your target is in cover or not, simply roll a die. On a 4+ it is not, on 3 or less it is.

Any dice that rolls a 1 is always a miss, regardless of modifiers. However, if modifiers to the roll mean that the unit would need more than 6 to hit, it can still use ranged attacks and will need 6 to hit, but it only rolls dice equal to half of its Attacks (rounding down).

DAMAGING THE TARGET

After discarding any dice that missed, pick up the dice and roll them again, to try and damage the enemy unit. The number your unit needs to damage the target is equal to the target's Defence value. This roll can sometimes be modified by special rules, etc.

Any die that rolls a 1 always fails to damage, regardless of modifiers. If a modifier brings the score required to damage a target to above 6, that target cannot be damaged.

Recording Damage

For each hit that scores damage, place a damage marker next to the unit. This represents physical damage and casualties as well as a decline in the unit's morale, cohesion and will to fight on.

As the unit accumulates damage markers, it might be more convenient to record this by writing it down, or placing a die (possibly an unusual one, of a different size or colour, to avoid rolling it by mistake) next to a single damage marker behind the unit, or using some other suitable tokens.

TESTING NERVE

At the end of the Shoot phase, test the Nerve of any unit you inflicted damage on in that phase. This test is described on page 68, and will determine whether the damaged units stand, waver or run away.

MELEE

When you're done shooting with all of your units, it's time for your warriors to strike against the enemies that they have charged that turn. Of course, in reality the enemy warriors would be striking against yours, but for the sake of playability we imagine that in your turn the impetus of the charge means that your men will be doing most of the hacking and slashing, while the enemy mostly defend themselves. If the enemy is not annihilated or routed, your men will fall back and brace themselves, for you can be sure that the enemy will charge back into the fight during their turn to avenge their fallen comrades.

At this stage, there will be a number of combats on the table equal to the number of enemy units you charged in the Move phase. Pick one of these combats and resolve it completely before moving to the next, and so on until all combats have been resolved.

STRIKING

To attack the unit you charged, roll a number of dice equal to the charging unit's Attacks value.

If your unit is attacking an enemy to the flank, it doubles its Attacks.

If your unit is attacking an enemy to the rear, it trebles its Attacks.

HITTING THE TARGET

This process is exactly the same as described for ranged attacks, except that it uses the unit's Melee value rather than the Ranged one, and the modifier below rather than the ones for shooting.

Modifiers

A number of factors can make a hit less likely to happen, such as a -1 modifier for Hindered charges (see below) or those from special rules.

For each of these factors, add or deduct the modifiers from the score rolled by the dice. For example, if your unit normally needs a 4 or more to hit, but is Hindered (-1 modifier), you will need 5 or more to hit instead. If you incur an additional -1 to hit, you would need 6s.

Any dice that rolls a 1 is always a miss, regardless of modifiers. However, if modifiers to the roll mean that the unit would need more than 6 to hit, it can still attack and will need 6 to hit, but it only rolls dice equal to half of its Attacks (rounding down).

Hindered Charges

If a charging unit's move has gone through or ended over any portion of difficult terrain or an obstacle then it is Hindered in the following melee phase. While Hindered, units suffer a -1 modifier when rolling to hit. A unit can only be Hindered once in any given charge, so will only ever suffer a single -1 modifier as a result of a Hindered charge.

A unit that is Counter-Charging is never Hindered, whether by terrain, special rules or any other method.

DAMAGING THE TARGET

This process is exactly the same as described for ranged attacks.

Recording Damage

This process is exactly the same as described for ranged attacks.

TESTING NERVE

At the end of each combat, if you have managed to score at least one point of Damage on the target, test the target's Nerve. This test is described on page 68, and will determine whether the damaged units stand, waver or run away.

REGROUP!

Target Destroyed – Chargers Regroup

At the end of each combat, if your unit(s) managed to rout the target, it can do one of the following:

- stay where it is and pivot around its centre to face any direction (as per a Change Facing order).

- move directly forward D6". The unit must move the full distance rolled. This move is not affected by difficult terrain and obstacles.

- move directly backwards D3" (as above).

A unit cannot move through any other units while regrouping, though it can pivot through them as long as it ends clear.

Once the Regroup move has been carried out, shuffle the unit so that there is a 1" gap between it and all enemy units, and so that it is not touching any friendly units. Move the unit the shortest distance possible in any direction to maintain the gap (usually this will be straight back 1" but use whichever direction is the shortest).

Target Remains – Chargers Pull Back

If, on the other hand, your unit did not manage to rout its enemies and is therefore still in contact with them, it must be moved directly back 1" – your warriors have been fought off and must fall back, close ranks and brace themselves for the inevitable counter-attack.

Remember at this point to separate any unit that ended up very close to other enemy units when charging the target, so that they are 1" apart once again. Also, make sure that your own units are separated by a little visible gap (a millimetre or so...).

If it is impossible to achieve the 1" distance from enemies, see if this can be done by moving said enemies away until they are 1" away. In the very rare cases when even this is impossible, then it's fine to leave them closer than 1".

DISORDERED

Units that have suffered at least one point of damage in the melee phase are Disordered – mark them with an appropriate counter.

They will remain disordered until the end of their following turn, when the Disordered counters are removed.

No Ranged Attacks

Disordered units cannot use any form of ranged attack (including magic). This is because they have been disrupted by the melee or are busy fighting back in close quarters.

NERVE

As a unit accumulates damage, it will become more and more likely to lose cohesion, until eventually it will turn tail and run from the field, never to return.

WHEN TO TEST

At the end of both the Move and Shoot phase of your turn, you test the Nerve of any enemy unit you managed to inflict damage upon during that phase. In the Melee phase, however, this test is done immediately at the end of each combat, if you managed to inflict damage on the target during that combat. In a combat where more than two units are involved, resolve all of the attacks first, and then take the Nerve test.

HOW TO TEST

Each unit has two numbers under its Nerve value. The first number is the unit's Wavering limit, the second number is its Routing limit.

To test the Nerve of an enemy unit, roll 2D6 and add to the result the points of damage currently on the unit, plus any other modifiers that apply (such as some special rules). This is the total you're using to 'attack' the enemy unit's Nerve. This total is then compared with the Nerve value of the enemy unit.

- If the total is equal to or higher than the unit's Routing limit, the unit suffers a Rout (see below).

- If the total is lower than the Routing limit, but equal to or higher than the Wavering limit, the unit suffers from a Wavering result (see below).

- If the total is lower than the unit's Wavering limit, then the unit is said to be Steady, which means it is completely unaffected and continues to fight on as normal.

For example, let's assume you are testing the Nerve of an enemy unit that has a Nerve of 11/13 and has suffered 3 points of damage. If you roll a seven or less, your total will be ten or less and the enemy will be Steady. If you roll an eight or nine, your total will be eleven or twelve and the enemy will be Wavering. If you roll a ten or more, the enemy Routs!

Steady

The unit continues to fight normally and does not suffer any negative effects. Remember however that units capable of ranged attacks, which have been Disordered will not be able to use their ranged attacks in their next turn.

Wavering

The unit does not rout, but is severely shaken during its next turn. In its next Move phase, it can only be given one of the following orders: Halt, Change Facing or Back. In addition, the unit is Disordered (so it will not be able to use its ranged attacks in its next Shoot phase).

It is normally a good idea to mark Wavering units with a token of some kind (like a bit of cotton wool).

Rout!

The unit routs of the field, is butchered to a man, or surrenders to the enemy and is taken prisoner – in any case, as far as this game is concerned, it is destroyed. Remove it.

EXCEPTIONAL MORALE RESULTS

Double Six – We Are Doomed!
If you roll double six when testing Nerve and the unit is not Routed, it will still suffer from a result of Wavering, as insidious news of defeat start to spread through the ranks.

Double One – Hold Your Ground!
If you roll snake eyes (double one) when testing Nerve, the enemy is filled with implacable resolve and will always be Steady and fight on, regardless of any modifier.

FEARLESS!

A few units in the game have a value of "-" for their Wavering Limit. For example, they could be -/14. These units are normally composed of fanatical, frenzied warriors or mindless supernatural creatures - in any case, they cannot Waver, and will therefore remain Steady until they eventually Rout.

Of course a routing result for such troops represents them being utterly annihilated, or collpasing as their magical lifeforce abandons them.

WAR ENGINES

Following are all of the exceptions that apply to War Engine units, unless differently specified in their entry.

Move

War Engines cannot be ordered to move At the Double, nor to Charge. While moving, War Engines treat obstacles as blocking terrain.

Melee

Attacking War Engines
Units attacking a War Engine always treble their Attacks, regardless of position.

Remember also that even if it survived such an onslaught, a War Engine would become Disordered as normal.

Shooting

Unless otherwise specified, War Engines have a range of 48".

Arc of Sight
If a War Engine's base is wider than 50mm, then its arc of sight is not taken from the corners. Instead the 50mm wide arc should be defined on the unit's base, such as by painting two vertical lines on the front or marking it with appropriate scenic decoration. It still has a front arc as normal, but when choosing a target for ranged attacks it may only choose one within the arc of sight taken from the 50mm marked on the base.

For example, the base shown right has an 80mm width, but the arc of sight only extends from a 50mm width on the front of the base.

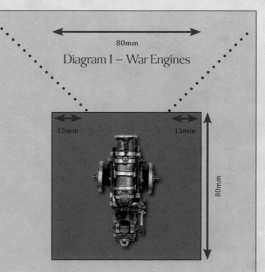

Diagram I – War Engines

INDIVIDUALS

Units with this rule are normally made of a single model representing a roughly man-sized individual, on foot or horseback. These obviously behave in a very different manner from regimented units or very large creatures. The following rules represent this:

Line of Sight

Before being given an order, an individual may pivot to face any direction for free.

Individuals never block line of sight or offer cover against ranged attacks.

Move

Individuals have the Nimble special rule.

Shooting

Individuals may pivot to face any direction for free before picking a target in the shooting phase.

Enemies shooting against Individuals suffer an additional -1 to hit modifier.

Melee

When charging an individual, a unit must make contact with the face that they started in as normal, however the Individual will turn to align flush with the unit's facing, rather than the unit aligning to the individual's facing.

Enemies never double/treble their Attacks when fighting the individual (including against Individual War Engines).

Similarly, the individual does not double/treble its own attacks when attacking an enemy in the flank/rear. It does still treble its attacks against war engines, however.

If an individual is routed and the charger (including another individual) decides to advance D6" directly forward, it can make contact with another enemy unit. This

is treated as a successful charge and the charger is lined up against the new enemy as normal and can immediately attack again!

If either the initial charge move or the regroup move took the charging unit over an obstacle or through difficult terrain, then it is hindered during this additional combat.

Also note that if the new enemy is another individual, which is then routed, the charger can again advance D6" forward as above, and so on – you can run over any number of meddling individuals in a single charge!

SPECIAL RULES

Some units, or even entire armies, possess what we call 'special rules'. Each of these special rules is an exception to the normal rules. Some are listed with the units themselves, but the most common are listed below.

Big Shield

If you are worried about not finding any cover, best bring it with you to the battle!

All attacks (ranged and melee) from enemies that are in the unit's front arc treat its defence as 6+.

Blast (n)

This rule is used for all weapons that explode on impact with the target or otherwise inflict massive amounts of damage with a single hit.

If the unit's attack hits the target, the target suffers a number of hits equal to the number in brackets, rather than a single hit.

For example, if a unit suffers a hit from a *Blast (D6+3)* attack, it will suffer from four to nine hits rather than a single one. Once this is done, roll for damage as normal for all of the hits caused.

Breath Attack (n)

This rule is used for dragon breath and other attacks where a great gout of flame or toxic gas fills an area.

The unit has a ranged attack for which you roll (n) dice rather than the Attacks value of the unit. This attack has a range of 12" and always hits on 4+, regardless of any modifier.

Sometimes this rule is listed as Breath Attack (Att). In this case use the unit's Attacks stat as the value for n.

Brutal

To be showered with the life fluids and innards of one's former comrades is a rather unnerving experience...

When testing the Nerve of an enemy unit in melee with one or more of your units with this rule, add +1 to the total.

Crushing Strength (n)

This rule is used to represent the devastating effects of melee hits from creatures of terrible strength or that are equipped with very heavy close combat weapons or even magical weaponry.

All melee hits inflicted by the unit have a +(n) modifier when rolling to damage.

Elite

Creatures with this rule are supremely skilled – true masters of the art of war.

Whenever the unit rolls to hit, it can re-roll all dice that score a natural, unmodified 1.

Ensnare

This rule is used to represent all of the means, both physiscal and supernatural, to slow down an enemy's momentum – from weighted nets to beguiling spells.

When attacking this unit in its front, enemies suffer an additional -1 to hit in melee.

Fly

This rule can literally represent flying movement (not really soaring high in the sky, however... more like fluttering around, a bit like a chicken), or even a ghostly creature's ability to move through solid matter.

The unit can move over anything (blocking terrain, enemy units, friendly units when charging, etc.), but still cannot land on top of them. The unit does not suffer hindered charges for moving over difficult terrain or obstacles, unless it ends the move within or touching them. The unit also has the *Nimble* special rule.

Fury

Some warriors and creatures are just too frenzied with bloodlust to ever slow down in their relentless assault.

While wavered, this unit may declare a Counter-Charge.

Headstrong

"Wavering's for little wide-eyed girls with ribbons in their hair... and Elves." – Dwarf proverb.

Whenever the unit begins a turn Wavering, it rolls a die. On a 4+ it shrugs off the effects of Wavering and is Disordered instead.

Indirect Fire

The unit fires its shots in high arcing trajectories, which means that the distance to the target is pretty much irrelevant and that most cover is pretty much useless. However, if any enemies get really close, it's impossible to hit them.

The unit fires in high arcs, hitting the target from the top, which means it does not suffers the –1 to hit modifier for cover.

On the other hand, the unit cannnot shoot targets that are within 12".

Note that the firing unit does still need to see its target to fire at it.

Individual

This rule is explained on page 71.

Inspiring

The bravery of a heroic general, or the presence of a great big flag, can convince warriors to stand their ground a little longer. For creatures like the undead (that don't care much about banners), the proximity of their general or of a sorcerous banner fills them with supernatural energy.

If this unit, or any friendly non-allied unit within 6" of this unit, is Routed, the opponent must re-roll that Nerve test. The second result stands.

Note a unit can also have Inspiring (specific unit) – in that case the unit will only inspire itself and that unit.

Iron Resolve

Some elite troops can hold their ground even when they have taken horrendous casualties.

If this unit is Steady as a result of a nerve test, it regains 1 point of damage previously suffered.

Lifeleech(n)

The blood and life energy of the enemy are sustainance for these unnatural creatures.

In a melee, this unit regains one point of damage it has previously suffered for every point of damage it deals, up to a maximum of n.

Nimble

Used for flyers, lightly armed units like skirmishers and scouting cavalry, and heroic individuals that venture on the battlefield on their own, this rule makes the unit considerably more manoeuvrable and more suited at using their ranged weapons to harass the enemy.

The unit can make a single extra pivot of up to 90 degrees around its centre while executing any move order, including a Charge! It cannot make this extra pivot when ordered to Halt.

In addition, the unit does not suffer from the −1 to hit modifier for moving and shooting.

Pathfinder

Mystical affinity to nature or simply a very good eye for terrain?

The unit suffers no movement penalties for difficult terrain, simply treating it as open terrain.

Pathfinder units are not Hindered for charging through difficult terrain.

Phalanx

From the front, these units look like a forest of sharp spikes pointing at you.

Units that charge this unit's front cannot use the Thunderous Charge special rule.

Piercing(n)

This rule is used for ranged attacks that can penetrate armour with ease (such as shots from rifles), as well as magical ranged attacks.

All ranged hits inflicted by the unit have a +(n) modifier when rolling to damage.

Regeneration(n)

Creatures gifted with this ability are very difficult to kill, as their wounds heal at incredible speed.

Every time this unit receives a move order (including Halt!), before doing anything else, roll a number of dice equal to the amount of damage currently on the unit. For every result of (n) or higher, the unit recovers a point of damage.

Reload!

Some powerful missile weapons take much longer to reload, making them less flexible.

The unit can fire only if it received a Halt order that turn.

Shambling

Braiiinsss... braiiiinnnssss...

The unit cannot be ordered 'At the Double', except when carrying out a Vanguard move.

Stealthy

The unit is extremely adept at hiding or benefits from magical protection that makes it very difficult to target with ranged attacks.

Enemies shooting against the unit suffer an additional -1 to hit modifier.

Strider

The unit is big enough or agile enough to brush past any barrier.

The unit never suffers the penalty for Hindered charges.

Thunderous Charge (n)

This rule is used for mounted knights equipped with lances and other units that rely on momentum to deliver a powerful charge.

All melee hits inflicted by the unit have a +(n) modifier when rolling to damage. This bonus is in addition to the unit's Crushing Strength (if any), however the unit loses this bonus when Disordered or during Hindered charges.

Vanguard

This unit is trained to range ahead of the main force, scouting the terrain and gathering information about the enemy.

The unit can make a single At the Double or Advance order after set-up is finished. If both armies have units with this rule, roll a die. The highest scorer decides who begins to move one of their *Vanguard* units first, then the players alternate until all *Vanguard* units have been moved.

Very Inspiring

The best leaders are able to command every unit on the battlefield by use of sorcery or numerous brave messengers.

This is the same as the *Inspiring* special rule, except that it has a range of 9". Any rule which affects *Inspiring* also affects *Very Inspiring*.

Vicious

The unit fights with utter ferocity, resorting to serrated blades and wicked hooks, eye gouging and all manner of other unsporting behaviour.

Whenever the unit rolls to damage, it can re-roll all dice that score a natural, unmodified 1.

Yellow Bellied

What did the boss-man say? It sounded like 'retreat'... yes, I'm pretty sure it was that...

When this unit wishes to charge an enemy unit's front facing, roll a die. If the result is a 1 then the unit 'misunderstands' the order and carries out a Halt! order instead.

This does not apply if the unit wishes to charge the flank or rear of an enemy unit, an individual or war engine, or if it is carrying out a Counter-Charge.

PICKING A FORCE

You can play *Kings of War* with just a few units per side, without worrying about the two sides being equally matched. This is great for learning the game, but after you've become familiar with the rules and have amassed a large collection of models, you might want to try a game where the forces facing one another across the battlefield are balanced, so that both players have an equal chance of winning the game.

In order to achieve this, you and your opponent must pick an army before the game. First agree a total of points, say for example 2,000 points. Then start picking units from one of the force lists provided in this book – each unit costs a certain amount of points, as listed in its entry in the appropriate force list (including any options like magical artefacts). For example a regiment will cost around 100 points.

As you pick them and include them in your army, keep adding their cost until you have reached the total you agreed. You can of course spend less than the agreed total, but you cannot spend even a single point more. However, an army is still considered to be the size of the maximum total the players agreed on (e.g. an army which come to 1995 points would still be considered a 2000 point army).

Army Selection

In order to restrict the possible (nasty) combinations that can be fielded and to make sure armies have a resemblance of 'realism' about them, we introduce the following limitations to the unit types that can make up your army:

Troops

Your army can include up to 2 Troops per Regiment in the army.

Your army can also include up to 4 Troops per Horde in the army.

Regiments

Your army can include as many Regiments as you like. For every Regiment in the army, you can also include the following:

  1 War Engine OR 1 Monster OR 1 Hero

For example, including 3 Regiments gives you access to up to 3 additional units chosen from War Engines, Heroes or Monsters.

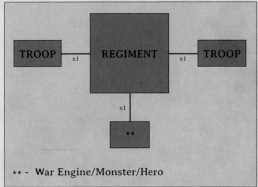

** - War Engine/Monster/Hero

Hordes

Your army can include as many Hordes as you like.

For every Horde in the army, you can also include the following:

  Up to 1 war engine and 1 hero and
  1 monster.

For example, including 3 Hordes gives you access to up to 3 additional War Engines, up to 3 additional Heroes AND up to 3 additional Monsters (see diagram overleaf).

Legions

Legions are Hordes for the purposes of army selection.

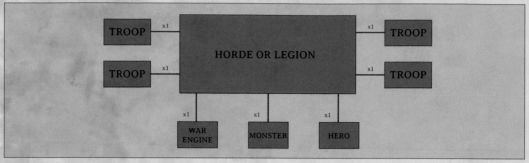

Irregular Units

Note that some units have an asterisk next to their name (for example: Gargoyles*). We call these *irregular units*, because they are not representative of the core, or mainstay force, of their army. This means that the unit is treated as a Troop from the point of view of Army Selection, even if it is a Regiment or Horde – i.e. it does not unlock any optional Troops, Heroes, Monsters or War Engines, and it needs to be unlocked by a Regiment, Horde or Legion of 'regular' troops.

Heroes (Monsters)

Heroes that belong to the Monster unit type (Hero (Mon)) simply count as a Hero from the point of view of force selection. So if you have a Horde, you can field a Hero (Mon) as well as a Monster.

Living Legends

In addition, if a unit has [1] after its name in the list, it is a Living Legend and this means that only one such unit exists and can therefore be included in an army. Of course it might happen that both opponents field this unit... in which case one of them must surely be an impostor and only the test of battle can show which one!

ALLIES & ALIGNMENTS

When using allies, you are free to mix units from different army lists in your army, as long as you always keep in mind that you need Regiment/Hordes of a specific army to include Troops, War Engines, Heroes or Monsters of that race, as normal.

If you are using allies then you may only choose up to 25% of your points limit from

Smaller Games

If you are a new player with a small model collection you sometimes want to throw a few units on the table to learn the game. You might even be running a small demo of the game for friends or even teaching the kids the joys of wargaming. Whatever the circumstances, you might want to consider allowing any number of Troops in an army when playing games below around 750 points. This allows both sides to field a decent variety on unit types and for players who are still collecting their armies to get them on the table and play some games.

the allied list. You may not take Living Legends as Allies. In addition, alliances between races that are hated enemies in the *Kings of War* background are not very 'realistic', so we have given a specific Alignment to each army – either Good, Evil or Neutral.

Good races should never ally with Evil races, but anybody can ally with Neutral races. So please don't mix Evil and Good units in the same army, unless your opponent agrees, of course. You can also join forces with your friends and play with several allied armies on either or both sides, as long as the points values are balanced.

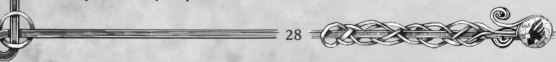

MAGICAL ARTEFACTS

Magical artefacts bestow bonuses to the unit they are given to. Each unit can have a single artefact chosen from the list below, which is normally carried by the unit's Leader. The cost of the artefact is added to that of the unit.

Unless the artefact specifies otherwise, the following limits also apply:

• Each artefact is unique and therefore can only be chosen once per army.

• War Engine units cannot choose artefacts.

• Monster units cannot choose artefacts. But Hero (Mon) units definitely can.

• Living Legends (i.e. units with a [1] limit) cannot choose artefacts.

Artefacts are magical in nature (some of them might even be sentient!), and all of them have the magical power of changing their shape. This allows them to morph into a weapon, piece of armour, jewel or other implement that is more akin to the race of the warrior carrying it. For example, a Blade of Slashing could be an elegant sword in the hands of an Elf, but will turn into a crude meat cleaver in the hands of an Orc. This magical property is of course very convenient from the point of view of the average war gamer!

As the presence of these items is not obvious, players must tell their opponent which artefact any of their units is carrying as they deploy them on the battlefield. If both players agree before deployment, you may want to play with 'hidden artefacts'. This is somewhat less fair, but can be considerably more fun...

When an item refers to 'normal' ranged attacks, it cannot be used with Breath Attack or Spells.

Blade of Slashing   Cost: 5 pts

Whenever the unit rolls to hit in Melee, it can re-roll one of the dice that failed to hit.

Fire-Oil   Cost: 5 pts

Against units with the Regeneration rule this unit gains an additional Piercing (1) on 'normal' ranged attacks, and Crushing Strength (1) in melee.

Kevinar's Flying Hammer   Cost: 5 pts

The unit has a ranged attack for which you roll a single die, regardless of the Attacks value of the unit. This attack has a range of 12" and always hits on 4+, regardless of modifiers, and if a hit is scored, it is resolved at Piercing (2).

Mace of Crushing   Cost: 5 pts

Whenever the unit rolls to damage in melee, it can re-roll one of the dice that failed to damage.

War-bow of Kaba   Cost: 5 pts

The unit has a ranged attack for which you roll a single die, regardless of the Attacks value of the unit. This attack has a range of 24" and, when rolling to hit, the unit uses a basic Ra value of 4+, regardless of its actual Ra value. The roll to hit is affected as normal by to-hit modifiers, and if a hit is scored, it is resolved at Piercing (1).

Dwarven Ale

Cost: 10 pts

The unit has the Headstrong special rule.

Myrddin's Amulet of the Fire-heart

Cost: 10 pts

Once per game, after using a ranged attack or spell, this unit may immediately use another different ranged attack or spell it possesses, against the same or a different target.

Piercing Arrow

Cost: 10 pts

Whenever the unit rolls to damage with a 'normal' ranged attack, it can re-roll one of the dice that failed to damage.

Quicksilver Rapier

Cost: 10 pts

This unit has +1 to hit when attacking individuals in melee.

Brew of Courage

Cost: 15 pts

When testing Nerve against this unit, the enemies suffer an additional -1 to their total.

Brew of Haste

Cost: 15 pts

The unit has +1 Speed.

Pipes of Terror

Cost: 15 pts

The unit has the Brutal special rule.

Blade of the Beast Slayer

Cost: 20 pts

This artefact can only be used by Heroes.

The Hero has Crushing Strength (2) when attacking large infantry, large cavalry, monsters or heroes who do not have the Individual special rule. If the Hero already has Crushing Strength, it is increased by 2 when attacking those same targets.

Darklord's Onyx Ring

Cost: 20 pts

This artefact can only be used by Heroes with the Regeneration rule. The unit's Regeneration value is increased by 1. For example, a unit with Regeneration (5+) now has Regeneration (4+).

Helm of Confidence   Cost: 20 pts

You must always re-roll a rout result for this unit even if they are not in range of a unit with inspiring.

Inspiring Talisman   Cost: 20 pts

This artefact can only be used by Heroes. The Hero has the Inspiring special rule.

Maccwar's Potion of the Caterpillar   Cost: 20 pts

The unit has the Pathfinder special rule.

Blessing of the Gods   Cost: 25 pts

The unit has the Elite special rule.

Chant of Hate   Cost: 25 pts

The unit has the Vicious special rule.

Kaba's Holy Hand Grenades   Cost: 25 pts

The unit has a ranged attack for which you roll a single die, regardless of the Attacks value of the unit.

This attack has a range of 12" and always hits on 4+, regardless of modifiers. The attack also has the Blast (D6) and Piercing (2) special rule.

Scarletmaw's Fenulian Amulet   Cost: 25 pts

Units with the Lightning Bolt spell only. This item increases the unit's Lightning Bolt (n) value by 2. For example, Lightning Bolt (3) becomes Lightning Bolt (5).

Boots of Levitation   Cost: 30 pts

This artefact can only be used by Heroes. The Hero can Advance and then shoot as if it had Halted that turn. It can also move At the Double and shoot as if it had Advanced that turn.

Brew of Strength   Cost: 30 pts

The unit has Crushing Strength (1), or if the unit already has Crushing Strength, it is increased by 1.

Crepognon's Scrying Gem of Zellak   Cost: 30 pts

When starting to deploy their units, your opponent must deploy D3+1 units instead of a single one.

Diadem of Dragon-kind   Cost: 30 pts

The unit has the Breath Attack (10) rule.

Healing Charm   Cost: 30 pts

This artefact can only be used by Heroes. The Hero has the Heal (3) spell.

Heart-seeking Chant   Cost: 30 pts

The unit's ranged attacks and spells have the Piercing (1) special rule, or if the unit already has Piercing, it is increased by 1.

Mreb's Grimoire of Unspeakable Darkness   Cost: 30 pts

Units with the Surge special rule only. This item increases the unit's Surge (n) value by 4. For example, Surge (8) becomes Surge (12).

The Boomstick   Cost: 30 pts

This artefact can only be used by Heroes. The Hero has the Lightning Bolt (3) spell.

Boots of the Seven Leagues   Cost: 35 pts

This artefact can only be used by a Hero with the Individual special rule. The Hero has the Vanguard special rule.

Ensorcelled Armour Cost: 35 pts

This artefact can only be used by Heroes. The Hero's Defence is improved by 1, to a maximum of 6+.

Jar of the Four Winds Cost: 35 pts

The unit's 'normal' ranged attacks gain 12" to their range.

Medallion of Life Cost: 35 pts

This artefact can only be used by Heroes. The Hero has the Regeneration(5+) special rule.

Orcsbain's Amulet of Thorns Cost: 35 pts

The unit has the Phalanx special rule.

The Fog Cost: 35 pts

The unit has the Stealthy special rule.

Wine of Elvenkind Cost: 40 pts

The unit has the Nimble special rule.

Wings of Honeymaze Cost: 40 pts

This artefact can only be used by a Hero with the Individual rule. The Hero has the Fly special rule and increases their speed to 10.

Brew of Keen-eyeness Cost: 45 pts

The unit has +1 to hit with 'normal' ranged attacks.

Brew of Sharpness Cost: 45 pts

The unit has +1 to hit in melee.

Crystal Pendant of Retribution Cost: 50 pts

When the unit is Routed, all units in base contact with it suffer 2D6 hits at Piercing (3). These hits are resolved by the player that Routed the unit with the Crystal, which now has to (grudgingly, we're sure) resolve the hits against their own unit(s). After the damage has been resolved, no Nerve test is taken by the damaged units – they proceed to Regroup, but cannot move directly forward D6" for their Regroup action, deterred by the huge explosion.

SPELLS

The spells listed below summarize in brief the wealth of subtly different magical powers wielded by the spellcasters of the world of Mantica, which we refer to with the generic term of 'Wizards'. A wizard is any unit that has access to the spells below, and not a unit that is equipped with a magical artefact that reproduces the effects of a spell (like the Boomstick, for example).

Spells are ranged attacks and thus follow the normal rules for shooting (e.g. a model that moves at the Double cannot use these powers that turn), with the exceptions listed below.

For spells, you always roll the number of dice indicated in the (n) value in the Wizard's entry for that spell, rather than the Att value of the Wizard itself. The Att value of the Wizard is only used if the model was to use a normal ranged attack, like a bow, instead of its spells.

Spells always hit on 4+, and ignore all to-hit modifiers for ranged attacks, including any modifiers from special rules. Note that re-rolls (like the one provided by the Elite rule), unlike modifiers, do apply.

Some spells can only target a friendly unit – this is marked as 'friendly unit only'. Note that such spells cannot normally target the wizard itself and cannot target friendly allied units – so a wizard from your main force can't bane chant an allied unit for example, and a wizard from your allied force can't heal a unit from your main force.

Each wizard's individual entry lists which spells can be purchased for him/her, much in the same way as equipment, and how much each additional spell is going to cost. This allows you to customise your wizards for your favourite battlefield role. Keep in mind, however, that a unit can make only a single shooting attack per turn, so buying more than one spell gives your wizard flexibility, as you can choose which one to use, but does not allow the Wizard to cast more than one spell per turn.

Spell	Range	Special Rules
Fireball (n)	12"	None – roll to damage as normal.
Bane-chant (n)	12"	Friendly unit only, including units engaged in combat. Hits don't inflict damage. Instead, if one or more hits are scored, for the rest of the turn all of the unit's melee and ranged attacks increase their Piercing and Crushing Strength value by 1, or gain Piercing (1) and Crushing Strength (1) if they don't already have these rules. Note that multiple bane-chants hitting the same unit do not have cumulative effects.
Wind Blast (n)	18"	Hits don't inflict damage. Instead, each hit pushes the target enemy unit 1" directly backwards if the caster is in the target unit's front arc, directly sideways and away from the caster if the caster is in either of the target unit's flank arcs, or directly forwards if the caster is in the target unit's rear arc. The target stops 1" away from enemy units or just out of contact with blocking terrain and friends. This spell has no effect on units with a speed of 0.
Lightning Bolt (n)	24"	Piercing (1) – roll to damage as normal.
Heal (n)	12"	Friendly unit only, including units engaged in combat. Hits don't inflict damage. Instead, for every hit 'inflicted', the friendly unit removes a point of damage that it has previously suffered.
Surge (n)	12"	Friendly unit with the Shambling special rule only. Hits don't inflict damage. Instead, for every hit 'inflicted', the Shambling friendly unit moves straight forward a full inch (stopping just out of contact from friendly units and blocking terrain). If this movement brings it into contact with an enemy unit, treat this as a successful charge against the enemy facing that has been contacted. However, the charged unit will not take any Nerve tests for any damage it might have taken previously in that Shoot phase. If the Surge move took the unit over an obstacle or through difficult terrain then it will be hindered in the ensuing combat as normal. This spell has no effect on units with a speed of 0.

GAME SCENARIOS

1) Prepare your Forces

First of all you and your opponent need to pick armies to an agreed total of points, using the process described in 'Picking a Force', on page 76.

2) Choose a Gaming Area

We assume that games of *Kings of War* will be played on a 6'x4' foot table or other flat surface, like a floor.

For larger games, we recommend an extra 3' of width for every 1000 points over 2000. For games with 1500 or fewer points, we recommend using a smaller board size, like 4'x4'.

3) Determine Scenario

So, how do you win the game? Each scenario has a different set of objectives to complete, as described below. To determine which scenario you and your opponent will play, roll a die:

D6	Type of Game
1	Kill!
2	Invade!
3	Dominate!
4	Pillage!
5	Loot!
6	Kill and Pillage!

4) Place Terrain

Before the game, it's a good idea if you and your opponent put some terrain on the battlefield. Arrange it in a sensible manner, trying to recreate a plausible landscape of the fantastic world your armies are battling in. Alternatively, find a third and neutral person to lay out the terrain for you.

During this stage it's vital that you agree what each piece of terrain is going to count as during the game – is it blocking terrain, an obstacle, a piece of decorative terrain or an area of difficult terrain?

5) Set-up

After rolling for the type of game and setting up the objectives/loot, if any, both players roll a die. The person scoring highest chooses one long edge of the battlefield as their own and then places one of their units on that side of the battlefield, more than 12" from the middle line (see Set-Up diagram overleaf). Their opponent then does the same on the opposite side of the table. The players keep alternating in doing this until they have placed all of their units onto the table.

6) Who Goes First?

Both you and your opponent roll a die. The highest scorer chooses whether they are going to have the first turn or give the first turn to their opponent instead. Game on!

7) Duration

The game lasts until each player has taken six turns. At the end of turn 6, one player rolls a die. On a 1-3 the game ends. On a 4-6 both players play an extra turn and then the game ends – work out the winner as described in the scenario conditions.

You can of course vary the number of turns you want to play for, or decide to play for a set amount of time instead (e.g. two hours), after which the game continues until each player has had the same number of turns. Alternatively, you could also play a Timed Game, as explained in the Timed Games section (page 39).

SCENARIO 1: KILL!

Objective

At the end of the game, add up the cost of all of enemy units you Routed. That is your score. Your opponent does the same and you compare scores.

If the difference between the scores in favour of a player is at least 10% of the total cost of the armies, that player wins, otherwise the game is a draw. For example, in a game where armies are 2,000 points, you need at least 200 points more than your opponent to win.

SCENARIO 2: INVADE!

Objective

At the end of the game, add up the cost of all of your units that are entirely inside the opponent's half of the table. That is your score. Your opponent does the same and you compare scores.

If the difference between the scores in favour of a player is at least 10% of the total cost of the armies, that player wins, otherwise the game is a draw. For example, in a game where armies are 2,000 points, you need at least 200 points more than your opponent to win.

SCENARIO 3: DOMINATE!

Objective

At the end of the game, add up the cost of all of your units that are entirely within 12" of the centre of the playing area. That is your score. Your opponent does the same and you compare scores.

If the difference between the scores in favour of a player is at least 10% of the total cost of the armies, that player wins, otherwise the game is a draw. For example, in a game where armies are 2,000 points, you need at least 200 points more than your opponent to win.

Set-Up Diagram

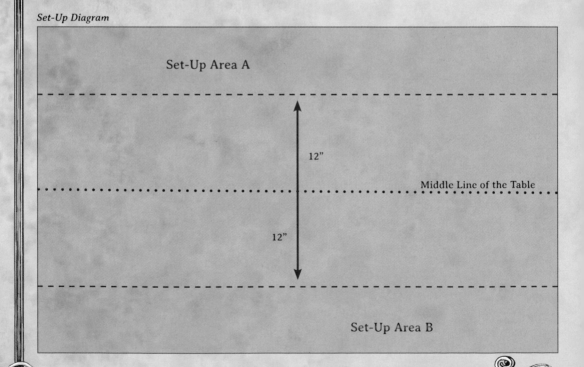

Scenario 4: Pillage!

Set-up

Place D3+4 objective markers on the battlefield before rolling for set-up. For objective markers you should use 25 mm round bases, but two pence coins or other items of similar size are also acceptable. Objective markers cannot be placed within Blocking Terrain.

Both players roll a die. Whoever scores highest places a marker anywhere on the battlefield. Players then take turns to place objective markers, which must be more than 12" apart from one another.

Objective

If, at the end of the game you have at least a unit within 3" of an objective and there are no enemy units within 3" of it, you control that objective. A single unit can control any number of objectives.

If you control more objectives than your opponent, you win, otherwise the game is a draw.

Individuals are always ignored from the point of view of controlling objectives (if it helps, remove them from the table before determining control of objectives).

Scenario 5: Loot!

Set-up

Before rolling for set up, place 3 loot markers on the battlefield (same size as objective markers); one in the dead centre of battlefield, and then the players each place one other loot marker on the centre line at least 12" away from other loot markers. Players dice off to determine who places their loot marker first. Loot Counters cannot be placed in Blocking Terrain.

Controlling Loot Markers

During the game, when one of your units **ends** its ends its move (excluding Vanguard moves) over a loot counter, it can pick it up. That unit will then carry the loot counter.

While carrying a loot counter, a unit's speed is reduced to 5 (unless it is already less than 5) and it cannot be targeted by Wind Blast or Surge.

A unit can drop any loot counters it is carrying at the start of any move - simply place the counter(s) anywhere in base contact with the unit and then move the unit as normal.

Units with one or more loot counters can leave the battle by moving into contact with their own table edge. If your unit leaves the battle it cannot return, but the loot counters it is carrying are safe.

If one of your units is Routed while carrying loot, place the counters anywhere within its footprint before removing the unit. If the unit was destroyed in a melee, your opponent automatically distributes the loot counters however they like among the units that are in contact with yours before your unit is removed.

Individuals cannot pick up nor carry the Loot – the best they can do is stand on a loot counter to defend it – as long as an individual is standing on a Loot counter, it cannot be picked up by the enemy.

Objective

At the end of the game you score one point for each loot counter in possession of one of your units, including those that have left the battle. If you score more points than your opponent, you win, otherwise the game is a draw.

SCENARIO 6: KILL AND PILLAGE!

Set-up

Follow the same process described for scenario 4: Pillage!

Objective

At the end of the game count the points just like in a Kill game. In addition to points for Routing units, however, any objective you control at the end of the game (as described in Pillage) is worth an amount of points equal to 10% of the total cost of the armies. For example, in a game where armies are 2,000 points, each objective is worth 200 points.

TIMED GAMES

We really enjoy playing *Kings of War* in a relaxed atmosphere, accompanied by epic music, beer, pizza and the unavoidable truculent banter. However, the game is designed so that you can also decide to introduce another dimension to the fight: time. This way you'll be able to experience some of the pressure of real battle, when snap decisions make the difference between victory or defeat, life or death!

Chess Clocks

The best tool for timed games is a chess clock, a device that ensures time is equally divided amongst the players, thus creating the ultimate fair and balanced war game.

Simply agree a number of turns for the game and an amount of time per player, and set the chess clock accordingly. For a 2,000 points game, we suggest six turns each and forty-five minutes per player, but it's up to you to find the pace you prefer for your games.

After deciding which player begins to set-up, start that player's clock. Once that player has set up their first unit, stop their clock, start their opponent's clock and so on. Once set-up is finished, stop both clocks and roll to see who has the first turn. Once the winner of the roll has made their choice, re-start that player's clock. That player plays a turn then stops their clock and activates the opponent's clock, and so on.

The game ends at the agreed number of turns and victory conditions are worked out as normal. However, if you happen to run out of time during one of your turns, the game ends instantly and your entire army routs – immediately remove all of your remaining units, as if they suffered a Rout result, and work out the victory conditions as normal. However, in an objective-based game (like 'Pillage' or 'Kill and Pillage', in the Scenarios section), your opponent is allowed to keep moving their units for as many turns as there are left in the game in order to grab objectives before the victory conditions are worked out.

Other Timers

If you don't have a chess clock at hand, don't worry – the stopwatch in your phone or watch, or even an hourglass or egg timer will do fine. If you use one of these, then each player gets an agreed amount of time per turn (agree first how many turns the game is going to last for). We suggest that each turn should take around two minutes per 500 points in your game (say 8 minutes in a 2,000 points game). If you run out of time during your turn, your move ends and any melee that has not been fought yet is cancelled – move the chargers back 1".

Make sure you set a time limit for set-up (30 seconds per unit works fine).

Be Nice!

Of course it's only fair to stop the chess clock or timer if one of the players is distracted from the game (by a phone call or the like), or if the players need to check a rule, an unclear line of sight, etc. It is also best if any unit you destroy during your turn is removed by the opponent, together with all of its damage markers, at the beginning of their turn.

By all means, you and your opponent can vary the amount of time you have for your game or your turns according to your own taste, but if you're like us, you are going to love the pressure created by timed games – after all, in real war one rarely has the luxury of time...

FORCE LISTS

FORCES OF BASILEA

Men-at-Arms (sword & shield) — Infantry

Unit Size	Sp	Me	Ra	De	Att	Ne	Pts
Troop (10)	5	4+	–	4+	10	10/12	80
Regiment (20)	5	4+	–	4+	12	14/16	115
Horde (40)	5	4+	–	4+	25	21/23	190

Men-at-Arms (spear & shield) — Infantry

Unit Size	Sp	Me	Ra	De	Att	Ne	Pts
Troop (10)	5	4+	–	4+	10	10/12	95
Regiment (20)	5	4+	–	4+	15	14/16	135
Horde (40)	5	4+	–	4+	30	21/23	225

Special
Phalanx

Crossbowmen — Infantry

Unit Size	Sp	Me	Ra	De	Att	Ne	Pts
Troop (10)	5	5+	5+	4+	8	10/12	100
Regiment (20)	5	5+	5+	4+	10	14/16	130
Horde (40)	5	5+	5+	4+	20	21/23	215

Special
Crossbows, Piercing (1), Reload!

Forces of Basilea Special Rules

Alignment: Good

Blessed Be The Pious
All units in this list have the Iron Resolve special rule, unless specified otherwise.

Penitents Mob — Infantry

Unit Size	Sp	Me	Ra	De	Att	Ne	Pts
Troop (10)	5	5+	–	3+	10	8/10	70
Regiment (20)	5	5+	–	3+	15	12/14	100
Horde (40)	5	5+	–	3+	30	19/21	165

Special
Crushing Strength (1), Headstrong

Paladin Foot Guard — Infantry

Unit Size	Sp	Me	Ra	De	Att	Ne	Pts
Troop (10)	5	3+	–	5+	10	11/13	105
Regiment (20)	5	3+	–	5+	12	15/17	150

Special
Headstrong

Options
• Exchange shields for two-handed weapons for free (lower Defence to 4+, gain Crushing Strength (1)

Paladin Knights — Cavalry

Unit Size	Sp	Me	Ra	De	Att	Ne	Pts
Troop (5)	8	3+	–	5+	8	12/14	135
Regiment (10)	8	3+	–	5+	16	15/17	210
Horde (20)	8	3+	–	5+	32	22/24	350

Special
Headstrong, Thunderous Charge (2)

Sisterhood Infantry — Infantry

Unit Size	Sp	Me	Ra	De	Att	Ne	Pts
Troop (10)	5	4+	–	3+	10	10/12	90
Regiment (20)	5	4+	–	3+	15	14/16	130
Horde (40)	5	4+	–	3+	30	21/23	215

Special

Crushing Strength (1), Headstrong, Vicious

Sisterhood Panther Lancers — Cavalry

Unit Size	Sp	Me	Ra	De	Att	Ne	Pts
Troop (5)	10	4+	–	3+	8	11/13	115
Regiment (10)	10	4+	–	3+	16	14/16	175

Special

Nimble, Thunderous Charge (1), Vicious

Sisterhood Panther Chariot — Large Cavalry

Unit Size	Sp	Me	Ra	De	Att	Ne	Pts
Regiment (3)	9	4+	–	4+	15	12/14	180
Horde (6)	9	4+	–	4+	30	15/17	280

Special

Base Size: 50x100mm, Thunderous Charge (2), Vicious

Heavy Arbalest — War Engine

Unit Size	Sp	Me	Ra	De	Att	Ne	Pts
1	5	–	5+	4+	1	10/12	65

Special

Blast (D3+2), *Reload!,* Piercing (3)

Elohi — Large Infantry

Unit Size	Sp	Me	Ra	De	Att	Ne	Pts
Regiment (3)	10	3+	–	5+	9	-/14	195
Horde (6)	10	3+	–	5+	18	-/17	300

Special

Crushing Strength (1), Fly, Inspiring, Thunderous Charge (1)

Phoenix — Monster

Unit Size	Sp	Me	Ra	De	Att	Ne	Pts
1	10	3+	–	3+	3	14/16	165

Special

Breath Attack (10), Crushing Strength (1), Fly, Heal (6), Inspiring, Regeneration (4+)

Dictator — Hero (Inf)

Unit Size	Sp	Me	Ra	De	Att	Ne	Pts
1	5	3+	–	5+	3	13/15	90

Special

Crushing Strength (1), Individual, Inspiring

Options

• Mount on a Basilean warhorse, increasing Speed to 8 and acquiring Thunderous Charge (1) (+30 pts), and changing to Hero (Cav)

Bearer of the Holy Icon — Hero (Inf)

Unit Size	Sp	Me	Ra	De	Att	Ne	Pts
1	5	5+	–	4+	1	10/12	55

Special

Individual, Inspiring

Options

• Mount on a barded horse, increasing Speed to 8 and Defense to 5+ (+20 pts), and changing to Hero (Cav)

Priest — Hero (Inf)

Unit Size	Sp	Me	Ra	De	Att	Ne	Pts
1	5	4+	–	4+	1	11/13	75

Special

Crushing Strength (1), Headstrong, Heal (3), Individual, Very Inspiring (Penitents only)

Options

• Bane-chant (2) for +15pts

• Mount on a horse, increasing Speed to 9 (+15 pts) and changing to Hero (Cav)

High Paladin Hero (Inf)

Unit Size	Sp	Me	Ra	De	Att	Ne	Pts
1	5	3+	–	5+	5	13/15	130

Special

Crushing Strength (1), Headstrong, Heal (2), Individual, Inspiring

Options

• Mount on a Basilean warhorse, increasing Speed to 8 and acquiring *Thunderous Charge (1)* (+30pts), and changing to Hero (Cav)

Abbess Hero (Inf)

Unit Size	Sp	Me	Ra	De	Att	Ne	Pts
1	5	3+	–	4+	4	12/14	90

Special

Crushing Strength (1), Headstrong, Individual, Very Inspiring (Sisterhood only), Vicious

Options

• Mount on a panther, increasing Speed to 10 and acquiring Thunderous Charge (1) (+20pts), and changing to Hero (Cav)

High Paladin on Griffin Hero (Mon)

Unit Size	Sp	Me	Ra	De	Att	Ne	Pts
1	10	3+	–	5+	7	15/17	210

Special

Crushing Strength (2), Fly, Headstrong, Heal (2), Inspiring

Abbess on Panther Chariot Hero (Lrg Cav)

Unit Size	Sp	Me	Ra	De	Att	Ne	Pts
1	9	3+	–	5+	8	14/16	170

Special

Base Size: 50x100mm, Crushing Strength (1), Headstrong, Thunderous Charge (1), Very Inspiring (Sisterhood only), Vicious

High Paladin on Dragon Hero (Mon)

Unit Size	Sp	Me	Ra	De	Att	Ne	Pts
1	10	3+	–	5+	9	17/19	310

Special

Base Size: 75x75mm, Breath Attack (10), Crushing Strength (3), Fly, Headstrong, Heal (2), Inspiring

Ur-Elohi Hero (Lrg Inf)

Unit Size	Sp	Me	Ra	De	Att	Ne	Pts
1	10	3+	–	5+	6	-/15	180

Special

Crushing Strength (2), Fly, Heal (3), Inspiring, Thunderous Charge (1)

War-Wizard
Hero (Inf)

Unit Size	Sp	Me	Ra	De	Att	Ne	Pts
1	5	4+	–	4+	1	11/13	60

Special

Fireball (8), Individual

Options

• Lightning Bolt (3) for +25 pts

• Wind Blast (5) for +30 pts

• Mount on a horse, increasing Speed to 9 (+15 pts) and changing to Hero (Cav)

Gnaeus Sallustis [1]
Hero (Lrg Cav)

Unit Size	Sp	Me	Ra	De	Att	Ne	Pts
1	9	3+	–	5+	7	15/17	190

Special

Crushing Strength (2), Headstrong, Heal (3),

Inspiring, Nimble

Jullius, Dragon of Heaven [1]
Hero (Lrg inf)

Unit Size	Sp	Me	Ra	De	Att	Ne	Pts
1	10	3+	–	6+	8	-/16	275

Special

Crushing Strength (2), Fly, Heal (3), Thunderous Charge (1), Twin Souls, Very Inspiring

Samacris, Mother of Phoenixes [1]
Hero (Lrg Inf)

Unit Size	Sp	Me	Ra	De	Att	Ne	Pts
1	10	3+	–	5+	3	-/15	230

Special

Fireball (10), Crushing Strength (1), Fly, Heal (7), Inspiring, Lightning Bolt (5), Regeneration (5+), Twin Souls

Twin Souls

As long as Samacris and Jullius are both present and in play on the table, they both have the Elite special rule.

DWARF ARMIES

Dwarf Army Special Rules

Alignment: Good

Grizzled Veterans
All units in this list have the *Headstrong* special rule, unless specified otherwise.

Dwarven Throwing Mastiffs
The Dwarfs train a breed of war-dog that is infamous for being even more vicious and hard-headed than its creators.

Mark a unit that has been equipped with throwing mastiffs with one or more such model. The unit has a ranged attack with a range of 12" that can be used only once per game (remove the mastiff markers once the weapon is used up).

When you release the hounds, roll 5 dice to hit, regardless of the firer's Attacks. Dogs always hit on 4+ regardless of modifiers. Then, for each point of damage caused, roll to hit and to damage again, as the surviving dogs savage the unfortunate opponents. Repeat this process again and again until you fail to score any damage, at which point even the toughest of the dogs have been put down or have run off to bury some of the enemies' limbs.

Against units with the *Shambling* special rule, you can re-roll any dice that fail to damage… the mastiffs are that keen.

Ironclad
Infantry

Unit Size	Sp	Me	Ra	De	Att	Ne	Pts
Troop (10)	4	4+	–	5+	10	10/12	75
Regiment (20)	4	4+	–	5+	12	14/16	110
Horde (40)	4	4+	–	5+	25	21/23	180

Options
- Dwarven Throwing Mastiff (+10 pts)

Ironguard
Infantry

Unit Size	Sp	Me	Ra	De	Att	Ne	Pts
Troop (10)	4	3+	–	6+	10	11/13	110
Regiment (20)	4	3+	–	6+	12	15/17	160

Options
- Exchange shields for two-handed weapons for free (lower Defence to 5+, gain Crushing Strength (1))
- Dwarven Throwing Mastiff (+10 pts)

Shieldbreakers
Infantry

Unit Size	Sp	Me	Ra	De	Att	Ne	Pts
Troop (10)	4	4+	–	4+	10	10/12	90
Regiment (20)	4	4+	–	4+	12	14/16	130
Horde (40)	4	4+	–	4+	25	21/23	215

Special
Crushing Strength (2)

Options
- Dwarven Throwing Mastiff (+10 pts)

Bulwarkers
Infantry

Unit Size	Sp	Me	Ra	De	Att	Ne	Pts
Troop (10)	4	4+	–	5+	10	10/12	105
Regiment (20)	4	4+	–	5+	15	14/16	150
Horde (40)	4	4+	–	5+	30	21/23	250

Special
Phalanx

Options
- Dwarven Throwing Mastiff (+10 pts)

Ironwatch Crossbows — Infantry

Unit Size	Sp	Me	Ra	De	Att	Ne	Pts
Troop (10)	4	5+	5+	4+	8	10/12	100
Regiment (20)	4	5+	5+	4+	10	14/16	135
Horde (40)	4	5+	5+	4+	20	21/23	225

Special
Crossbows, Piercing (1), Reload!

Ironwatch Rifles — Infantry

Unit Size	Sp	Me	Ra	De	Att	Ne	Pts
Troop (10)	4	5+	5+	4+	8	10/12	115
Regiment (20)	4	5+	5+	4+	10	14/16	155
Horde (40)	4	5+	5+	4+	20	21/23	255

Special
Rifles, Piercing (2), Reload!

Rangers — Infantry

Unit Size	Sp	Me	Ra	De	Att	Ne	Pts
Troop (10)	5	4+	4+	4+	10	10/12	135
Regiment (20)	5	4+	4+	4+	12	14/16	180

Special
Light crossbows (treat as bows), Crushing Strength (1), Pathfinder, Vanguard

Options
• Dwarven Throwing Mastiff (+10 pts)

Sharpshooters — Infantry

Unit Size	Sp	Me	Ra	De	Att	Ne	Pts
Troop (5)	4	5+	4+	5+	5	9/11	100

Special
Base Size: 25x50mm, Long rifles, Piercing (2),
Reload!

Berserkers — Infantry

Unit Size	Sp	Me	Ra	De	Att	Ne	Pts
Troop (10)	5	4+	–	3+	20	-/16	125
Regiment (20)	5	4+	–	3+	25	-/22	180

Berserker Brock Riders — Cavalry

Unit Size	Sp	Me	Ra	De	Att	Ne	Pts
Troop (5)	8	4+	–	4+	13	-/16	135
Regiment (10)	8	4+	–	4+	26	-/22	210

Special
Thunderous Charge (1), Vicious

Earth Elementals — Large Infantry

Unit Size	Sp	Me	Ra	De	Att	Ne	Pts
Regiment (3)	5	4+	–	6+	9	-/14	130
Horde (6)	5	4+	–	6+	18	-/17	200

Special
Crushing Strength (1), Pathfinder, Shambling

Greater Earth Elemental — Monster

Unit Size	Sp	Me	Ra	De	Att	Ne	Pts
1	5	4+	–	6+	8	-/18	160

Special
Crushing Strength (3), Pathfinder, Shambling

Ironbelcher Cannon — War Engine

Unit Size	Sp	Me	Ra	De	Att	Ne	Pts
1	4	–	5+	5+	1	10/12	110

Special
Blast (D6+2), Piercing (4), Reload!

While within 6" of a Friendly Warsmith, the unit has Blast (D6+3) instead.

Ironbelcher Organ Gun — War Engine

Unit Size	Sp	Me	Ra	De	Att	Ne	Pts
1	4	–	5+	5+	15	10/12	85

Special
Range 24", Piercing (2), Reload!

While within 6" of a Friendly Warsmith, the unit also has the Elite special rule.

Flame Belcher — War Engine

Unit Size	Sp	Me	Ra	De	Att	Ne	Pts
1	4	–	–	5+	18	10/12	85

Special

Breath Attack (Att).

While within 6" of a Friendly Warsmith, the unit also has the Elite special rule.

Jarrun Bombard — War Engine

Unit Size	Sp	Me	Ra	De	Att	Ne	Pts
1	4	–	5+	5+	1	10/12	110

Special

Blast (D6+3), Lob it!, Piercing (2), Reload!

Lob It!

The Bombard can be fired directly, as normal. Alternatively, you can choose to fire it indirectly, following the Indirect Fire special rule. When firing indirectly, the Bombard has a range of 60", but cannot be fired against targets within 12".

Battle Driller — Monster

Unit Size	Sp	Me	Ra	De	Att	Ne	Pts
1	4	4+	–	5+	D6+6*	10/12	70

Special

Base Size: 25x50mm, Height 1, Brutal, Crushing Strength (1), Individual

* Roll for the number of Attacks every time you resolve a melee.

Steel Behemoth — Monster

Unit Size	Sp	Me	Ra	De	Att	Ne	Pts
1	4	5+	–	6+	D6+20*	18/20	250

Special

Base Size: 50x100mm, Breath Attack (10), Crushing Strength (3)

*Roll for the number of Attacks every time you resolve a melee

King — Hero (Inf)

Unit Size	Sp	Me	Ra	De	Att	Ne	Pts
1	4	3+	–	6+	5	13/15	120

Special

Crushing Strength (1), Individual, Inspiring

King on Large Beast — Hero (Lrg Cav)

Unit Size	Sp	Me	Ra	De	Att	Ne	Pts
1	7	3+	–	6+	7	13/15	170

Special

Crushing Strength (1), Thunderous Charge (2), Inspiring

Warsmith — Hero (Inf)

Unit Size	Sp	Me	Ra	De	Att	Ne	Pts
1	4	4+	4+	5+	2	11/13	85

Special

Pistol, Crushing Strength (1), Individual, Inspiring (War Engines only), Piercing (1)

Army Standard Bearer — Hero (Inf)

Unit Size	Sp	Me	Ra	De	Att	Ne	Pts
1	4	5+	–	5+	1	10/12	50

Special

Individual, Inspiring

Ranger Captain — Hero (Inf)

Unit Size	Sp	Me	Ra	De	Att	Ne	Pts
1	5	3+	4+	5+	3	11/13	90

Special

Light crossbow (treat as bow), Crushing Strength (1), Individual, Inspiring (Rangers only), Pathfinder, Vanguard

Berserker Lord — Hero (Inf)

Unit Size	Sp	Me	Ra	De	Att	Ne	Pts
1	5	3+	–	4+	8	-/17	120

Special

Crushing Strength (1), Individual, Inspiring (Berserkers only)

Options

• Mount on a Brock (+30 pts), increasing Speed to 8, gaining Vicious and changing to Hero (Cav).

Stone Priest — Hero (Inf)

Unit Size	Sp	Me	Ra	De	Att	Ne	Pts
1	4	4+	–	5+	2	11/13	105

Special

Individual, Inspiring (Earth Elementals only), Surge (8)

Options

• Bane Chant (2) for +15 pts

Sveri Egilax [1] — Hero (Lrg Cav)

Unit Size	Sp	Me	Ra	De	At	Ne	Pts
1	8	3+	–	4+	10	-/19	240

Special

Crushing Strength (1), Elite, Inspiring, Thunderous Charge (1), Vicious

Herneas the Hunter [1] — Hero (Inf)

Unit Size	Sp	Me	Ra	De	At	Ne	Pts
1	5	3+	3+	5+	3	12/14	140

Special

Skewerer, Crushing Strength (2), Individual, Inspiring (Rangers only), Pathfinder, Stealthy, Vanguard

Skewerer

The Skewerer is a magic crossbow that in rules terms is treated as a bow with Piercing (3).

Leader of the Hunt

If your army includes Herneas, you may upgrade one unit of Rangers to represent his handpicked Ranger patrol (+20 pts). This unit has the Elite and Stealthy special rules.

Garrek Heavyhand [1] — Hero (Inf)

Unit Size	Sp	Me	Ra	De	At	Ne	Pts
1	4	3+	–	6+	5	14/16	150

Special

Warp Hammer, Shield of Miph, Individual, Inspiring

Warp Hammer

The bearer has Crushing Strength (3).

Shield of Miph

The bearer has Regeneration (6+).

ELF ARMIES

Elf Army Special Rules

Alignment: Good

Battle Hardened

All units in this list have Elite, unless specified otherwise.

Elven Sabre-Toothed Pussycat
Meeoww!

Mark a Hero that is accompanied by a sabre-toothed pussycat with an Elven cat model. The Hero has a ranged attack with a range of 12" that can be used only once per game (remove the cat once it has been unleashed).

This weapon can only be used against Heroes or Monsters, War Engines and Troops. The cat, with typical feline obedience, refuses to attack any body of troops larger than that.

When you send the cat to seek its prey, roll 5 dice to hit, regardless of the firer's Attacks. The cat always hits on 4+, regardless of modifiers, and has the *Piercing (1)* rule. Then, for any point of damage caused, roll to hit and to damage again, as the cat has its way with the victims. Repeat this process again and again until you fail to score any damage, at which point the cat has been slain or has wandered off to lick the gore off its paws.

Kindred Tallspears — Infantry

Unit Size	Sp	Me	Ra	De	Att	Ne	Pts
Troop (10)	6	4+	–	4+	10	10/12	100
Regiment (20)	6	4+	–	4+	15	14/16	140
Horde (40)	6	4+	–	4+	30	21/23	230

Special
Phalanx

Palace Guard — Infantry

Unit Size	Sp	Me	Ra	De	Att	Ne	Pts
Troop (10)	6	3+	–	4+	10	11/13	105
Regiment (20)	6	3+	–	4+	12	15/17	150

Special
Crushing Strength (1)

Therennian Sea Guard — Infantry

Unit Size	Sp	Me	Ra	De	Att	Ne	Pts
Regiment (20)	6	4+	5+	4+	12	14/16	170
Horde (40)	6	4+	5+	4+	25	21/23	280

Special
Bows, Phalanx

Kindred Archers — Infantry

Unit Size	Sp	Me	Ra	De	Att	Ne	Pts
Troop (10)	6	5+	4+	4+	8	10/12	115
Regiment (20)	6	5+	4+	4+	10	14/16	150
Horde (40)	6	5+	4+	4+	20	21/23	250

Special
Bows

Kindred Gladestalkers — Infantry

Unit Size	Sp	Me	Ra	De	Att	Ne	Pts
Troop (10)	6	4+	4+	3+	8	10/12	130
Regiment (20)	6	4+	4+	3+	10	14/16	175

Special
Bows, Pathfinder, Vanguard

Hunters of the Wild — Infantry

Unit Size	Sp	Me	Ra	De	Att	Ne	Pts
Troop (10)	6	4+	–	4+	20	10/12	135
Regiment (20)	6	4+	–	4+	25	14/16	190

Special

Vanguard, Pathfinder. This unit is not Elite.

Forest Shamblers — Large Infantry

Unit Size	Sp	Me	Ra	De	Att	Ne	Pts
Regiment (3)	6	4+	–	5+	9	–/14	125
Horde (6)	6	4+	–	5+	18	–/17	190

Special

Crushing Strength (1), Pathfinder, Shambling, Vanguard. This unit is not Elite.

Stormwind Cavalry — Cavalry

Unit Size	Sp	Me	Ra	De	Att	Ne	Pts
Troop (5)	9	3+	–	5+	8	11/13	140
Regiment (10)	9	3+	–	5+	16	14/16	215

Special

Thunderous Charge (2)

Silverbreeze Cavalry — Cavalry

Unit Size	Sp	Me	Ra	De	Att	Ne	Pts
Troop (5)	10	5+	4+	4+	7	11/13	145

Special

Bows, Nimble

Drakon Riders — Large Cavalry

Unit Size	Sp	Me	Ra	De	Att	Ne	Pts
Regiment (3)	10	3+	–	5+	9	12/14	175
Horde (6)	10	3+	–	5+	18	15/17	270

Special

Crushing Strength (1), Fly, Thunderous Charge (1)

War Chariots — Large Cavalry

Unit Size	Sp	Me	Ra	De	Att	Ne	Pts
Regiment (3)	8	4+	4+	4+	8	12/14	140
Horde (6)	8	4+	4+	4+	16	15/17	215

Special

Bows, Base Size: 50x100mm, Thunderous Charge (2)

Bolt Thrower — War Engine

Unit Size	Sp	Me	Ra	De	Att	Ne	Pts
1	6	–	4+	4+	2	10/12	90

Special

Blast (D3), Piercing (2), Reload!

Dragon Breath — War Engine

Unit Size	Sp	Me	Ra	De	Att	Ne	Pts
1	6	–	4+	4+	15	10/12	90

Special

Breath Attack (Att)

Elven King Hero (Inf)

Unit Size	Sp	Me	Ra	De	Att	Ne	Pts
1	6	3+	–	5+	5	13/15	120

Special

Crushing Strength (1), Individual, Inspiring

Options

• Mount on a horse, increasing Speed to 9 (+20 pts) and changing to Hero (Cav)

• Sabre-Toothed Pussycat (+10 pts)

Army Standard Bearer Hero (Inf)

Unit Size	Sp	Me	Ra	De	Att	Ne	Pts
1	6	5+	–	4+	1	10/12	50

Special

Individual, Inspiring

Options

• Mount on a horse, increasing Speed to 9 (+15 pts) and changing to Hero (Cav)

Drakon Rider Lord Hero (Lrg Cav)

Unit Size	Sp	Me	Ra	De	Att	Ne	Pts
1	10	3+	–	5+	5	13/15	160

Special

Crushing Strength (1), Fly, Inspiring, Thunderous Charge (1),

Elven Mage Hero (Inf)

Unit Size	Sp	Me	Ra	De	Att	Ne	Pts
1	6	5+	–	4+	1	10/12	75

Special

Heal (3), Individual

Options

• Lightning Bolt (5) for +45 pts

• Wind Blast (5) for +30 pts

• Fireball (10) for +10 pts

• Bane Chant (2) for +15 pts

• Mount on a horse, increasing Speed to 9 (+15 pts) and changing to Hero (Cav)

• Sabre-Toothed Pussycat (+10 pts)

Dragon Kindred Lord Hero (Mon)

Unit Size	Sp	Me	Ra	De	Att	Ne	Pts
1	10	3+	–	5+	10	17/19	310

Special

Breath Attack (15), Crushing Strength (3), Fly, Inspiring

Elven Prince Hero (Inf)

Unit Size	Sp	Me	Ra	De	Att	Ne	Pts
1	6	3+	–	5+	3	11/13	60

Special

Crushing Strength (1), Individual

Options

• Mount on a horse, increasing Speed to 9 (+15 pts) and changing to Hero (Cav)

• Sabre-Toothed Pussycat (+10 pts)

Master Hunter Hero (Inf)

Unit Size	Sp	Me	Ra	De	Att	Ne	Pts
1	7	3+	3+	4+	3	11/13	90

Special

Bow, Individual, Pathfinder, Piercing (1), Stealthy, Vanguard

Options

• Sabre-Toothed Pussycat (+10 pts)

Forest Warden Hero (Lrg Inf)

Unit Size	Sp	Me	Ra	De	Att	Ne	Pts
1	6	4+	–	5+	3	11/13	75

Special

Crushing Strength (2), Nimble, Pathfinder, Vanguard. A Forest Warden is not Elite.

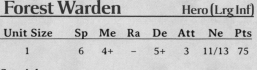

Noble War Chariot Hero (Lrg Cav)

Unit Size	Sp	Me	Ra	De	Att	Ne	Pts
1	8	3+	4+	4+	4	11/13	90

Special

Bow, Base Size: 50x100mm, Thunderous Charge (2)

Tree Herder — Hero (Mon)

Unit Size	Sp	Me	Ra	De	Att	Ne	Pts
1	6	3+	–	6+	7	18/20	260

Special
Crushing Strength (3), Inspiring, Pathfinder, Surge (8), Vanguard. A Tree Herder is not Elite.

Argus Rodinar [1] — Hero (Inf)

Unit Size	Sp	Me	Ra	De	At	Ne	Pts
1	0	-	–	5+	–	-/13	50

Special
Base Size: 50x50mm, Altar of the Elements, Individual

Altar of the Elements
Argus Rodinar treats all Wavering results as Steady and is never disordered by chargers – he is protected by powerful enchantments.

The Altar has a spell which automatically hits any one friendly non-allied unit on the battlefield, regardless of range or line of sight. Any nerve tests against this unit that result in a rout must be re-rolled, as if it were in range of an Inspiring unit. This spell lasts until the start of your next turn. Remember that dice cannot be re-rolled more than once.

The Green Lady [1] — Hero (Inf)

Unit Size	Sp	Me	Ra	De	At	Ne	Pts
1	10	–	–	6+	–	14/16	200

Special
Fly, Heal (8), Individual, Inspiring, Pathfinder, Regeneration (5+)

Options
• Up to 2 Sabre-Toothed Pussycats (+10 pts each)

The Wild Guard
If your army includes the Green Lady, for +20 points you may upgrade a single Regiment of Hunters of the Wild to represent the Green Lady's Wild Guard, her most devoted and sworn guardians. This unit has the Headstrong and Regeneration (5+) special rules.

KINGDOMS OF MEN

Kingdoms of Men Special Rules

Alignment: Neutral

Rallying Cry
All units in this list with the Inspiring rule have the Very Inspiring rule instead (already noted in their profile), including Inspiring granted by other means such as Magical Artefacts.

Shield Wall — Infantry

Unit Size	Sp	Me	Ra	De	Att	Ne	Pts
Troop (10)	5	4+	–	4+	10	9/11	70
Regiment (20)	5	4+	–	4+	12	13/15	100
Horde (40)	5	4+	–	4+	25	20/22	165

Foot Guard — Infantry

Unit Size	Sp	Me	Ra	De	Att	Ne	Pts
Troop (10)	5	3+	–	5+	10	10/12	95
Regiment (20)	5	3+	–	5+	12	14/16	135
Horde (40)	5	3+	–	5+	25	21/23	225

Options
• Exchange shields for two-handed weapons for free (lower Defence to 4+, gain Crushing Strength (1))

Pike Block — Infantry

Unit Size	Sp	Me	Ra	De	Att	Ne	Pts
Regiment (20)	5	4+	–	3+	15	13/15	135
Horde (40)	5	4+	–	3+	30	20/22	225

Special
Ensnare, Phalanx

Heavy Pike Block — Infantry

Unit Size	Sp	Me	Ra	De	Att	Ne	Pts
Regiment (20)	5	4+	–	4+	15	14/16	165
Horde (40)	5	4+	–	4+	30	21/23	270

Special
Elite, Ensnare, Phalanx

Spear Phalanx — Infantry

Unit Size	Sp	Me	Ra	De	Att	Ne	Pts
Troop (10)	5	4+	–	4+	10	9/11	85
Regiment (20)	5	4+	–	4+	15	13/15	120
Horde (40)	5	4+	–	4+	30	20/22	200

Special
Phalanx

Pole-Arms Block — Infantry

Unit Size	Sp	Me	Ra	De	Att	Ne	Pts
Troop (10)	5	4+	–	3+	10	9/11	70
Regiment (20)	5	4+	–	3+	12	13/15	100
Horde (40)	5	4+	–	3+	25	20/22	165

Special
Crushing Strength (1)

Militia Mob*   Infantry

Unit Size	Sp	Me	Ra	De	Att	Ne	Pts
Troop (10)	5	5+	–	3+	10	8/10	50
Regiment (20)	5	5+	–	3+	12	12/14	70
Horde (40)	5	5+	–	3+	25	19/21	115
Legion (60)	5	5+	–	3+	30	25/27	170

Berserkers   Infantry

Unit Size	Sp	Me	Ra	De	Att	Ne	Pts
Troop (10)	5	3+	–	3+	10	-/12	100
Regiment (20)	5	3+	–	3+	15	-/16	140
Horde (40)	5	3+	–	3+	30	-/23	230

Special
Crushing Strength (1)

Bowmen   Infantry

Unit Size	Sp	Me	Ra	De	Att	Ne	Pts
Troop (10)	5	5+	5+	3+	8	9/11	75
Regiment (20)	5	5+	5+	3+	10	13/15	100
Horde (40)	5	5+	5+	3+	20	20/22	165

Special
Bows

Crossbowmen   Infantry

Unit Size	Sp	Me	Ra	De	Att	Ne	Pts
Troop (10)	5	5+	5+	3+	8	9/11	85
Regiment (20)	5	5+	5+	3+	10	13/15	115
Horde (40)	5	5+	5+	3+	20	20/22	190

Special
Crossbows, Piercing (1), Reload!

Arquebusiers   Infantry

Unit Size	Sp	Me	Ra	De	Att	Ne	Pts
Troop (10)	5	5+	5+	3+	8	9/11	100
Regiment (20)	5	5+	5+	3+	10	13/15	135
Horde (40)	5	5+	5+	3+	20	20/22	225

Special
Rifles, Piercing (2), Reload!

Knights   Cavalry

Unit Size	Sp	Me	Ra	De	Att	Ne	Pts
Troop (5)	8	3+	–	5+	8	11/13	125
Regiment (10)	8	3+	–	5+	16	14/16	195
Horde (20)	8	3+	–	5+	32	21/23	340

Special
Headstrong, Thunderous Charge (2)

Mounted Scouts   Cavalry

Unit Size	Sp	Me	Ra	De	Att	Ne	Pts
Troop (5)	9	5+	5+	3+	7	10/12	100

Special
Bows, Nimble

Options
- Exchange bows with pistols for free (gain Piercing (1) but halve their range) or exchange bows with carbines for +15 pts (gain Piercing (1) and range 18").

Mounted Sergeants   Cavalry

Unit Size	Sp	Me	Ra	De	Att	Ne	Pts
Troop (5)	9	4+	–	4+	7	10/12	105
Regiment (10)	9	4+	–	4+	14	13/15	160

Special
Nimble, Thunderous Charge (1)

Charioteers   Large Cavalry

Unit Size	Sp	Me	Ra	De	Att	Ne	Pts
Regiment (3)	8	4+	5+	4+	8	11/13	115
Horde (6)	8	4+	5+	4+	16	14/16	175

Special
Bows, Base Size: 50x100mm, Thunderous Charge (2)

Cannon   War Engine

Unit Size	Sp	Me	Ra	De	Att	Ne	Pts
1	5	–	5+	4+	1	9/11	85

Special
Blast (D6+1), Piercing (4), Reload!

Siege Artillery — War Engine

Unit Size	Sp	Me	Ra	De	Att	Ne	Pts
1	5	–	5+	4+	1	9/11	90

Special

Blast (D6+2), Indirect Fire, Piercing (3), Reload!

Ballista — War Engine

Unit Size	Sp	Me	Ra	De	Att	Ne	Pts
1	5	–	5+	4+	1	9/11	60

Special

Blast (D3+2), Piercing (3), Reload!

Beast of War — Monster

Unit Size	Sp	Me	Ra	De	Att	Ne	Pts
1	7	4+	-	5+	12	15/17	210

Special

Base Size: 50x100mm, Brutal, Crushing Strength (2), Thunderous Charge (2)

Options

• Mount a light ballista on it (+10 pts) – Range 36", Ra 5+, 2 attacks, Blast (D3), Piercing (2)

General — Hero (Inf)

Unit Size	Sp	Me	Ra	De	Att	Ne	Pts
1	5	3+	–	5+	4	12/14	100

Special

Crushing Strength (1), Individual, Very Inspiring

Options

• Mount on a horse, increasing Speed to 8 (+20 pts) and changing to Hero (Cav), or mount on a Pegasus, increasing Speed to 10 and gaining Fly, but losing the Individual special rule (+50 pts) and changing to Hero (Large Cav).

General on Winged Beast — Hero (Mon)

Unit Size	Sp	Me	Ra	De	Att	Ne	Pts
1	10	3+	–	5+	6	14/16	190

Special

Crushing Strength (2), Fly, Very Inspiring

Hero — Hero (Inf)

Unit Size	Sp	Me	Ra	De	Att	Ne	Pts
1	5	3+	–	5+	3	10/12	50

Special

Crushing Strength (1), Individual

Options

• Mount on a horse, increasing Speed to 8 (+15 pts) and changing to Hero (Cav), or mount on a Pegasus, increasing Speed to 10 and gaining Fly, but losing the Individual special rule (+40 pts) and changing to Hero (Large Cav).

Army Standard Bearer — Hero (Inf)

Unit Size	Sp	Me	Ra	De	Att	Ne	Pts
1	5	5+	–	4+	1	9/11	50

Special
Individual, Very Inspiring

Options
• Mount on a horse, increasing Speed to 9 (+15 pts) and changing to Hero (Cav)

Wizard — Hero (Inf)

Unit Size	Sp	Me	Ra	De	Att	Ne	Pts
1	5	4+	–	4+	1	10/12	50

Special
Fireball (6), Individual

Options
• Lightning Bolt (3) for +25 pts, or free if it replaces Fireball
• Wind Blast (5) for +30 pts
• Bane Chant (2) for +15 pts
• Heal (2) for +10 pts
• Mount on a horse, increasing Speed to 9 (+15 pts) and changing to Hero (Cav), or mount on a Pegasus, increasing Speed to 10 and gaining Fly, but losing the Individual special rule (+25 pts) and changing to Hero (Large Cav).

The Captain [1] — Hero (Inf)

Unit Size	Sp	Me	Ra	De	At	Ne	Pts
1	5	3+	–	5+	3	11/13	150

Special
Crushing Strength (1), Individual, Master Tactician, Very Inspiring

Options
• Mount on a horse, increasing Speed to 8 (+20 pts) and changing to Hero (Cav).

Master Tactician
You can redeploy D3 of your own units after deployment is finished, but before vanguard moves are made.

FORCES OF NATURE

Naiad Ensnarers — Infantry

Unit Size	Sp	Me	Ra	De	Att	Ne	Pts
Troop (10)	5	4+	–	3+	10	9/11	100
Regiment (20)	5	4+	–	3+	12	13/15	140
Horde (40)	5	4+	–	3+	25	20/22	230

Special

Ensnare, Regeneration (4+)

Naiad Heartpiercers — Infantry

Unit Size	Sp	Me	Ra	De	Att	Ne	Pts
Troop (10)	5	5+	4+	3+	8	9/11	120
Regiment (20)	5	5+	4+	3+	10	13/15	160

Special

Harpoon-gun, Piercing (1), Regeneration (4+)

Naiad Wyrmriders — Large Cavalry

Unit Size	Sp	Me	Ra	De	Att	Ne	Pts
Regiment (3)	8	3+	–	4+	9	12/14	155
Horde (6)	8	3+	–	4+	18	15/17	240

Special

Crushing Strength (1), Regeneration (4+), Thunderous Charge (1)

Hunters of the Wild — Infantry

Unit Size	Sp	Me	Ra	De	Att	Ne	Pts
Troop (10)	6	4+	–	4+	20	10/12	135
Regiment (20)	6	4+	–	4+	25	14/16	190

Special

Vanguard

Forces of Nature Special Rules

Alignment: Neutral

Creatures of Nature

All units in this list have the *Pathfinder* special rule, unless specified otherwise.

Wild Companions

A Wild Companion is a feral animal that is bound by magical means to a Druid or other master of the natural lore, or simply allied or in thrall to a particular race or creature.

Mark units that are accompanied by a Wild Companion with a suitable model – a panther, bear, wolf, hawk, etc. The unit then can unleash the beast once per game. This is the same as using a Fireball (5) spell with Piercing (1) – remove the animal model once it has been unleashed.

Centaur Bray-Striders — Cavalry

Unit Size	Sp	Me	Ra	De	Att	Ne	Pts
Troop (5)	8	3+	–	4+	6	11/13	100
Regiment (10)	8	3+	–	4+	12	14/16	155

Special

Crushing Strength (1), Thunderous Charge (1)

Centaur Bray-Hunters — Cavalry

Unit Size	Sp	Me	Ra	De	Att	Ne	Pts
Troop (5)	8	4+	5+	3+	6	11/13	105
Regiment (10)	8	4+	5+	3+	12	14/16	165

Special

Bows, Nimble, Thunderous Charge (1)

Salamanders — Infantry

Unit Size	Sp	Me	Ra	De	Att	Ne	Pts
Troop (10)	5	4+	–	5+	10	10/12	100
Regiment (20)	5	4+	–	5+	12	14/16	140
Horde (40)	5	4+	–	5+	25	21/23	230

Special
Base Size: 25x25mm, Crushing Strength (1)

Options
• Exchange shields for two-handed weapons for free (lower Defence to 4+, gain Crushing Strength (2))

Sylph Talonriders * — Large Cavalry

Unit Size	Sp	Me	Ra	De	Att	Ne	Pts
Regiment (3)	10	4+	4+	3+	6	12/14	135
Horde (6)	10	4+	4+	3+	12	15/17	210

Special
Bows, Fly

Forest Shamblers — Large Infantry

Unit Size	Sp	Me	Ra	De	Att	Ne	Pts
Regiment (3)	6	4+	–	5+	9	-/14	125
Horde (6)	6	4+	–	5+	18	-/17	190

Special
Crushing Strength (1), Shambling, Vanguard.

Hydra — Monster

Unit Size	Sp	Me	Ra	De	Att	Ne	Pts
1	6	4+	–	5+	5*	15/17	140

Special
Crushing Strength (2), Regeneration (5+)

*Multiple heads – in addition to the basic 5, the Hydra has a number of additional attacks equal to its current points of Damage.

Beast of Nature — Monster

Unit Size	Sp	Me	Ra	De	Att	Ne	Pts
1	7	3+	–	5+	5	15/17	130

Special
Crushing Strength (2)

Options
• Lightning Bolt (6) for +30pts
• Breath Attack (10) for +15pts
• Fly and Speed 10 for +50pts
• Vicious and increase Attacks to 7 for +30pts

Elementals — Large Infantry

Unit Size	Sp	Me	Ra	De	Att	Ne	Pts
Regiment (3)	5	4+	–	5+	9	-/14	130
Horde (6)	5	4+	–	5+	18	-/17	200

Special
Crushing Strength (1), Shambling.

Options
MUST take one of the following options:
• Earth: become De 6+ for free
• Fire: become Sp 6 and Crushing Strength (2) for free
• Air: become Sp 10 and gain Fly, but lose Crushing Strength for +20pts
• Water: become Sp 7 and gain Regeneration (5+) for +20pts

Greater Elemental — Monster

Unit Size	Sp	Me	Ra	De	Att	Ne	Pts
1	5	4+	–	5+	8	-/18	160

Special
Crushing Strength (2), Shambling

Options
MUST take one of the following options:
• Earth: become De 6+ and Crushing Strength (3) for free
• Fire: become Sp 6 and Crushing Strength (4), and gain Breath Attack (6) for free
• Air: become Sp 10 and gain Fly and Wind Blast (3) but reduced to Crushing Strength (1) for +30pts
• Water: become Sp 7 and gain Regeneration (5+) for +30pts

Druid
Hero (Inf)

Unit Size	Sp	Me	Ra	De	Att	Ne	Pts
1	5	5+	–	4+	1	10/12	65

Special
Heal (2), Individual, Inspiring

Options
- Lightning Bolt (3) for +20pts
- Wind Blast (5) for +30pts
- Surge (7) for +40pts
- Bane-chant (2) for +15pts
- Can ride a stag, horse, lesser unicorn or similar mount, increasing Speed to 9, for +15 pts and changing to Hero (Cav)
- Up to two Wild Companions (+10 pts each)

Forest Warden
Hero (Large Inf)

Unit Size	Sp	Me	Ra	De	Att	Ne	Pts
1	6	4+	–	5+	3	11/13	75

Special
Crushing Strength (2), Nimble, Vanguard

Tree Herder
Hero (Mon)

Unit Size	Sp	Me	Ra	De	Att	Ne	Pts
1	6	3+	–	6+	7	18/20	260

Special
Crushing Strength (3), Inspiring, Surge (8), Vanguard

Centaur Chief
Hero (Cav)

Unit Size	Sp	Me	Ra	De	Att	Ne	Pts
1	8	3+	–	4+	4	11/13	105

Special
Crushing Strength (2), Thunderous Charge (1), Inspiring, Individual

Options
- Bow gaining Ra 4+ for +10pts
- Wild Companion (+10 pts)

Naiad Stalker
Hero (Inf)

Unit Size	Sp	Me	Ra	De	Att	Ne	Pts
1	6	3+	–	4+	4	11/13	90

Special
Crushing Strength (1), Individual, Inspiring (Naiads only), Regeneration (4+), Stealthy

Options
- Harpoon-gun, gaining Ra 4+ and Piercing (1) for +20pts
- Wild Companion for +10 pts

Salamander Veteran
Hero (Inf)

Unit Size	Sp	Me	Ra	De	Att	Ne	Pts
1	5	3+	-	5+	4	11/13	85

Special
Base Size: 25x25mm, Crushing Strength (2), Individual, Inspiring (Salamanders only)

Options
- Wild Companion for +10 pts

Winged Unicorn
Hero (Lrg Cav)

Unit Size	Sp	Me	Ra	De	Att	Ne	Pts
1	10	3+	–	5+	4	12/14	170

Special

Fly, Heal (7), Inspiring, Thunderous Charge (2)

Options

• Lightning Bolt (5) for +20pts

• Wind Blast (5) for +20pts

• Bane-chant (2) for +15pts

Unicorn
Hero (Cav)

Unit Size	Sp	Me	Ra	De	Att	Ne	Pts
1	10	3+	–	5+	3	11/13	120

Special

Heal (5), Individual, Thunderous Charge (2)

Pegasus
Hero (Lrg Cav)

Unit Size	Sp	Me	Ra	De	Att	Ne	Pts
1	10	3+	–	4+	3	10/12	80

Special

Fly, Thunderous Charge (1)

The Green Lady [1]
Hero (Inf)

Unit Size	Sp	Me	Ra	De	At	Ne	Pts
1	10	–	–	6+	–	14/16	200

Special

Elite, Fly, Heal (8), Individual, Inspiring,
Regeneration (5+)

Options

• Up to 2 Wild Companions (+10pts each)

The Wild Guard

The Wild Guard are the most devoted guardians of
the Green Lady, sworn to protect her and to uphold
her ideals until death takes them.

If your army includes the Green Lady, for +20 points
you may upgrade a single Regiment of Hunters of the
Wild to represent the Green Lady's Wild Guard, her
most devoted and sworn guardians. This unit has the
Headstrong and Regeneration (5+) special rules.

Keris [1]
Hero (Inf)

Unit Size	Sp	Me	Ra	De	Att	Ne	Pts
1	5	4+	–	4+	1	12/14	160

Special

Fireball (7), Heal (1), Individual, Inspiring, Lightning
Bolt (2), Solar Staff, Surge (8)

Options

• Can be accompanied by Ozzee (Wild Companion)
for +10 pts

Solar staff

The bearer has a single ranged attack with a range of
24" that always hits on 4+ (regardless of modifiers).
If the target unit is hit, it is blinded until the end of
its following Shoot phase – place a suitable marker
next to the target. As long as it's blinded, the unit
cannot Charge and is Disordered.

Shaarlyot [1]
Hero (Inf)

Unit Size	Sp	Me	Ra	De	Att	Ne	Pts
1	10	4+	–	3+	1	12/14	150

Special

Fireball (10), Fly, Individual, Inspiring,
Wind Blast (7)

Options

• Can be accompanied by Tiffee (Wild Companion)
for +10 pts

OGRE ARMIES

Ogre Army Special Rules

Alignment: Neutral

Hammer Blow
All units in this list have the Brutal special rule, unless specified otherwise.

Note: Red Goblin units are not Brutal, but on the other hand neither are they 'Yellow Bellied' – it's the thought of what would happen to them if they disobeyed their Ogre masters.

Warriors · Large Infantry

Unit Size	Sp	Me	Ra	De	Att	Ne	Pts
Regiment (3)	6	3+	–	5+	9	12/14	130
Horde (6)	6	3+	–	5+	18	15/17	200
Legion (12)	6	3+	–	5+	36	22/24	350

Special
Crushing Strength (1)

Options
• Exchange shields with two-handed weapons for free (lower Defence to 4+, but gain Crushing Strength (2))

Berserker Braves · Large Infantry

Unit Size	Sp	Me	Ra	De	Att	Ne	Pts
Regiment (3)	6	4+	–	4+	15	-/15	150
Horde (6)	6	4+	–	4+	30	-/18	230

Special
Crushing Strength (1)

Siege Breakers · Large Infantry

Unit Size	Sp	Me	Ra	De	Att	Ne	Pts
Regiment (3)	5	3+	–	4+	9	12/14	165
Horde (6)	5	3+	–	4+	18	15/17	250

Special
Big Shield, Crushing Strength (3), Thunderous Charge (1)

Hunters · Large Infantry

Unit Size	Sp	Me	Ra	De	Att	Ne	Pts
Regiment (3)	6	3+	–	4+	9	12/14	145
Horde (6)	6	3+	–	4+	18	15/17	220

Special
Crushing Strength (1), Ensnare, Pathfinder

Shooters · Large Infantry

Unit Size	Sp	Me	Ra	De	Att	Ne	Pts
Regiment (3)	6	4+	5+	4+	9	12/14	150
Horde (6)	6	4+	5+	4+	18	15/17	230

Special
Heavy crossbows, Crushing Strength (1), Piercing (2), Reload!

Boomers · Large Infantry

Unit Size	Sp	Me	Ra	De	Att	Ne	Pts
Regiment (3)	6	4+	-	4+	9	12/14	150
Horde (6)	6	4+	-	4+	18	15/17	230

Special
Breath Attack (Att), Crushing Strength (1), Piercing (1)

Chariots
Large Cavalry

Unit Size	Sp	Me	Ra	De	Att	Ne	Pts
Regiment (3)	7	3+	–	5+	12	12/14	170
Horde (6)	7	3+	–	5+	24	15/17	265

Special

Base Size: 50x100mm, Crushing Strength (1),
Thunderous Charge (2)

Red Goblins *
Infantry

Unit Size	Sp	Me	Ra	De	Att	Ne	Pts
Regiment (20)	5	6+	5+	3+	10	12/14	85
Horde (40)	5	6+	5+	3+	20	19/21	140

Special

Bows

Red Goblin Scouts *
Cavalry

Unit Size	Sp	Me	Ra	De	Att	Ne	Pts
Troop (5)	10	4+	-	4+	7	9/11	100
Regiment (10)	10	4+	-	4+	14	12/14	155

Special

Thunderous Charge (1), Nimble

Red Goblin Blaster
Monster

Unit Size	Sp	Me	Ra	De	Att	Ne	Pts
1	5	–	–	5+	*	8/10	65

Special

Base Size: 50x100mm, Height 3

The Red Goblin operator (whose model, by the way, is always ignored) can trigger the Blaster explosion at any point during any of its Shoot phases, even if it has moved At The Double or is Disordered that turn – all units (friend and foe) within D6" of the Blaster model suffer 2D6 hits with Piercing (4), and then the Blaster model is immediately Routed. Roll the number of hits once, but then roll to damage individually for each unit hit. Friendly units taking damage as a result do not have to take Nerve tests, but enemy units will do as normal.

If a Blaster routs as a result of a Nerve test, it explodes as above.

*If a Blaster charges an enemy unit, it will simply detonate in the Shoot phase as above.

Mammoth
Monster

Unit Size	Sp	Me	Ra	De	Att	Ne	Pts
1	7	4+	–	5+	12	15/17	210

Special

Base Size: 50x100mm, Crushing Strength (2),
Thundering Charge (2)

Options

• Mount a Ballista on it: Range 36", Ra 5+,
  2 Ranged Attacks, Blast (D3), Piercing (2) for +10 pts

Giant
Monster

Unit Size	Sp	Me	Ra	De	Att	Ne	Pts
1	7	4+	–	5+	(D6+6)*	17/19	190

Special

Fury, Crushing Strength (3), Strider

* Roll for the number of Attacks every time you resolve a melee

Warlord
Hero (Lrg Inf)

Unit Size	Sp	Me	Ra	De	Att	Ne	Pts
1	6	3+	–	5+	7	15/17	175

Special

Crushing Strength (2), Inspiring, Nimble

Options

• Exchange shield with two-handed weapon for free
  (lower Defence to 4+, but gain Crushing Strength (3)).
• Mount on chariot for +15 pts, gaining Thunderous
  Charge (2) and Speed 7, but losing Nimble and
  changing to Hero (Large Cav) on a 50x100mm base.

Captain
Hero (Lrg Inf)

Unit Size	Sp	Me	Ra	De	Att	Ne	Pts
1	6	3+	5+	5+	5	13/15	135

Special

Crushing Strength (2), Inspiring, Nimble

Options

• Exchange shield with two-handed weapon for free
  (lower Defence to 4+, but gain Crushing Strength (3)).
• Exchange shield with heavy crossbow (gain Reload!
  and Piercing (2), but lower Defence to 4+), for
  +10pts.
• Mount on chariot for +15 pts, gaining Thunderous
  Charge (2) and Speed 7, but losing Nimble and
  changing to Hero (Large Cav) on a 50x100mm base.

Army Standard Hero (Lrg Inf)

Unit Size	Sp	Me	Ra	De	Att	Ne	Pts
1	6	3+	–	4+	3	11/13	70

Special

Crushing Strength (1), Inspiring, Nimble

Options

• Mount on chariot for +15 pts (gain Thunderous Charge (2), Defence 5+ and Speed 7, but losing Nimble) and changing to Hero (Large Cav) on a 50x100mm base.

Warlock Hero (Lrg Inf)

Unit Size	Sp	Me	Ra	De	Att	Ne	Pts
1	6	4+	–	4+	2	12/14	100

Special

Crushing Strength (1), Inspiring (Berserker Braves only), Lightning Bolt (3), Nimble.

In addition, the Warlock gains an additional dice for spells for each unit of Berserker Braves within 6".

Options

Fireball (12) for +30pts

Wind Blast (5) for +30pts

Boomer Sergeant Hero (Lrg Inf)

Unit Size	Sp	Me	Ra	De	Att	Ne	Pts
1	6	4+	–	4+	4	11/13	90

Special

Breath Attack (Att), Crushing Strength (1), Nimble, Piercing (1)

Siege Master Hero (Lrg Inf)

Unit Size	Sp	Me	Ra	De	Att	Ne	Pts
1	5	3+	–	4+	4	12/14	135

Special

Big Shield, Crushing Strength (3), Inspiring (Siege Breakers only), Nimble, Thunderous Charge (1)

Red Goblin Biggit Hero (Inf)

Unit Size	Sp	Me	Ra	De	Att	Ne	Pts
1	5	4+	4+	4+	3	9/11	60

Special

Bow, Individual, Inspiring (Red Goblin units only)

Options

• Mount on a Fleabag, increasing Speed to 10 (+15 pts and changing to Hero (Cav)

Grokagamok [1] Hero (Lrg Inf)

Unit Size	Sp	Me	Ra	De	Att	Ne	Pts
1	6	3+	–	5+	7	15/17	260

Special

The Amputator, Crushing Strength (3), Nimble, Very Inspiring

The Amputator

The bearer of this massive axe has an increased Crushing Strength (already included in the profile).

In addition, the bearer's Melee attacks also have the Blast (D3) special rule.

FORCES OF THE ABYSS

Forces of the Abyss Special Rules

Alignment: Evil

Abyssal Vengeance
All units in this list have Fury, unless specified otherwise.

Abyssal Guard

Infantry

Unit Size	Sp	Me	Ra	De	Att	Ne	Pts
Troop (10)	5	3+	–	5+	10	11/13	110
Regiment (20)	5	3+	–	5+	12	15/17	160

Special
Regeneration (5+)

Options
• Exchange shields for two-handed weapons for free (lower Defence to 4+, gain Crushing Strength (1)

Larvae *

Infantry

Unit Size	Sp	Me	Ra	De	Att	Ne	Pts
Horde (40)	5	6+	–	4+	25	-/22	130
Legion (60)	5	6+	–	4+	30	-/28	190

Special
Ensnare, Shambling

Flamebearers

Infantry

Unit Size	Sp	Me	Ra	De	Att	Ne	Pts
Troop (10)	5	5+	4+	3+	8	10/12	105
Regiment (20)	5	5+	4+	3+	10	14/16	140

Special
Firebolts, Piercing (1), Regeneration (5+)

Lower Abyssals

Infantry

Unit Size	Sp	Me	Ra	De	Att	Ne	Pts
Troop (10)	5	4+	–	4+	10	10/12	85
Regiment (20)	5	4+	–	4+	12	14/16	120
Horde (40)	5	4+	–	4+	25	21/23	200

Special
Regeneration (5+)

Options
• Exchange shields for two-handed weapons for free (lower Defence to 3+, gain Crushing Strength (1)

Gargoyles *

Infantry

Unit Size	Sp	Me	Ra	De	Att	Ne	Pts
Troop (10)	10	4+	–	3+	8	9/11	80

Special
Base Sizes: 25x25mm, Fly, Regeneration (3+), Vicious
Note: this unit does not have the Fury special rule.

Succubi

Infantry

Unit Size	Sp	Me	Ra	De	Att	Ne	Pts
Troop (10)	6	3+	–	3+	20	10/12	135
Regiment (20)	6	3+	–	3+	25	14/16	190

Special
Ensnare, Stealthy.

Fleshlings Infantry

Unit Size	Sp	Me	Ra	De	Att	Ne	Pts
Troop (10)	5	5+	–	4+	10	10/12	65
Regiment (20)	5	5+	–	4+	12	14/16	90
Horde (40)	5	5+	–	4+	25	21/23	150

Options
• Exchange shields for two-handed weapons for free (lower Defence to 3+, gain Crushing Strength (1))

Hellhounds Cavalry

Unit Size	Sp	Me	Ra	De	Att	Ne	Pts
Troop (5)	9	4+	–	4+	15	10/12	125

Special
Height 1, Nimble, Thunderous Charge (1)

Abyssal Horsemen Cavalry

Unit Size	Sp	Me	Ra	De	Att	Ne	Pts
Troop (5)	8	3+	–	5+	9	11/13	140
Regiment (10)	8	3+	–	5+	18	14/16	215

Special
Crushing Strength (1), Thunderous Charge (1)

Imps * Large Infantry

Unit Size	Sp	Me	Ra	De	Att	Ne	Pts
Regiment (3)	5	5+	–	3+	12	11/13	70
Horde (6)	5	5+	–	3+	24	14/16	105

Special
Height 0, Vicious

Tortured Souls Large Infantry

Unit Size	Sp	Me	Ra	De	Att	Ne	Pts
Regiment (3)	10	4+	–	4+	9	-/15	145
Horde (6)	10	4+	–	4+	18	-/18	220

Special
Crushing Strength (2), Fly, Lifeleech (2), Shambling

Molochs Large Infantry

Unit Size	Sp	Me	Ra	De	Att	Ne	Pts
Regiment (3)	5	4+	–	4+	12	12/15	130
Horde (6)	5	4+	–	4+	24	15/18	200

Special
Base Size: 50x50mm, Crushing Strength (2), Brutal

Chroneas Monster

Unit Size	Sp	Me	Ra	De	Att	Ne	Pts
1	5	-	–	5+	-	16/18	210

Special
Breath Attack (20), Pathfinder, Piercing (1), Tempus (this unit cannot be Disordered)

Abyssal Champion Hero (Inf)

Unit Size	Sp	Me	Ra	De	Att	Ne	Pts
1	5	3+	–	5+	5	13/15	135

Special
Crushing Strength (1), Individual, Inspiring, Regeneration (5+).

Options
• Can have wings for +40 pts (gaining Fly and increasing Speed to 10)
• Lightning Bolt (5), for +40pts
• Can ride an abyssal mount, increasing Speed to 8, for +20 pts and changing to Hero (Cav)

Abyssal Temptress Hero (Inf)

Unit Size	Sp	Me	Ra	De	Att	Ne	Pts
1	6	3+	–	4+	5	11/13	90

Special
Ensnare, Individual, Inspiring (Succubi only), Stealthy

Options
• Bane Chant (2) for +15 pts
• Wind Blast (6) for +30 pts
• Can have wings for +30 pts (gaining Fly and increasing Speed to 10)

Efreet
Hero (Inf)

Unit Size	Sp	Me	Ra	De	Att	Ne	Pts
1	7	4+	–	4+	1	11/13	135

Special

Fireball (20), Individual, Pathfinder

Abyssal Harbinger
Hero (Inf)

Unit Size	Sp	Me	Ra	De	Att	Ne	Pts
1	5	5+	4+	4+	1	10/12	60

Special

Firebolt, Individual, Inspiring, Piercing (1),
Regeneration (5+).

Options

• Can ride an abyssal mount, increasing Speed to 8,
for +15 pts and changing to Hero (Cav)

Archfiend of the Abyss
Hero (Mon)

Unit Size	Sp	Me	Ra	De	Att	Ne	Pts
1	7	3+	–	5+	9	16/18	250

Special

Brutal, Crushing Strength (2), Inspiring,
Thunderous Charge (2), Vicious

Options

• Can have wings, gaining Fly and increasing Speed
to 10 for +50 pts
• Lightning Bolt (5), for +25pts

Ba'su'su the Vile [1]
Hero (Inf)

Unit Size	Sp	Me	Ra	De	Att	Ne	Pts
1	10	3+	–	5+	8	15/17	220

Special

Base Size: 25x25mm, Crushing Strength (2),
Fly, Individual, Inspiring (Gargoyles only),
Regeneration (5+), Vicious

Vile Spawn

If your army includes Ba'su'su, for +20 pts you may
upgrade a single unit of Gargoyles to represent his
flock of elder Gargoyles. This unit has Defence 4+ and
Crushing Strength (1).

The Lord of Lies [1]
Hero (Lrg Inf)

Unit Size	Sp	Me	Ra	De	Att	Ne	Pts
1	10	3+	–	5+	5	15/20	300

Special

Crushing Strength (2), Ensnare, Fly, Inspiring,
Lightning Bolt (7), Stealthy, Thunderous Charge (2)

The Well of Souls [1]
Hero (Mon)

Unit Size	Sp	Me	Ra	De	Att	Ne	Pts
1	10	4+	–	5+	10	-/20	275

Special

Crushing Strength (2), Fly, Inspiring, Lifeleech (5),
Shambling, Soul Drain

Soul Drain

The Well of Souls pulls the life force from the enemy
and feeds the Abyssal army. When the Well of Souls is
given an order, it may take up to 20 points of damage
on itself. However, this cannot take it to more than
20 damage in total. For each point of damage taken in
this way, it may remove one point of damage from a
friendly non-Allied unit within 9". The Well of Souls
will not take a nerve test for damage taken in this way.

ABYSSAL DWARFS

Abyssal Dwarfs Special Rules

Alignment: Evil

Cruel Masters
All units in this list have the Vicious special rule, unless specified otherwise.

Mutated Throwing Mastiffs
The Abyssal Dwarfs engage in wicked (but admittedly quite amusing) alchemically-adjusted cross-breeding of the traditional Dwarven Throwing Mastiff with all sorts of monstrous creatures.

Mutated Throwing Mastiffs are the same as Dwarven Throwing Mastiffs, except they re-roll failed rolls to damage against all enemies.

Immortal Guard   Infantry

Unit Size	Sp	Me	Ra	De	Att	Ne	Pts
Troop (10)	4	3+	–	5+	10	-/13	100
Regiment (20)	4	3+	–	5+	12	-/17	145

Options
• Mutated Throwing Mastiff (+15 pts)

• Exchange shields for two-handed weapons for free (lower Defence to 4+, gain Crushing Strength (1))

Decimators   Infantry

Unit Size	Sp	Me	Ra	De	Att	Ne	Pts
Troop (10)	4	5+	–	4+	10	10/12	120
Regiment (20)	4	5+	–	4+	12	14/16	160
Horde (40)	4	5+	–	4+	25	21/23	255

Special
Breath Attack (Att), Piercing (1)

Blacksouls   Infantry

Unit Size	Sp	Me	Ra	De	Att	Ne	Pts
Troop (10)	4	4+	–	5+	10	10/12	80
Regiment (20)	4	4+	–	5+	12	14/16	115
Horde (40)	4	4+	–	5+	25	21/23	190

Options
• Mutated Throwing Mastiff (+15 pts)

• Exchange shields for two-handed weapons for free (lower Defence to 4+, gain Crushing Strength (1))

Slave Orcs *   Infantry

Unit Size	Sp	Me	Ra	De	Att	Ne	Pts
Troop (10)	5	4+	–	4+	10	9/11	65
Regiment (20)	5	4+	–	4+	12	13/15	90
Horde (40)	5	4+	–	4+	25	20/22	150

Special
Base Size: 25x25mm, Crushing Strength (1), Yellow-Bellied, *Slave Orcs are not Vicious*

Abyssal Berserkers   Infantry

Unit Size	Sp	Me	Ra	De	Att	Ne	Pts
Troop (10)	5	4+	–	3+	20	-/13	125
Regiment (20)	5	4+	–	3+	25	-/17	180

Special
Crushing Strength (1)

Slave Orc Gore Riders *   Cavalry

Unit Size	Sp	Me	Ra	De	At	Ne	Pts
Troop (5)	8	4+	–	4+	8	9/11	85
Regiment (10)	8	4+	–	4+	16	12/14	130

Special
Crushing Strength (1), Thunderous Charge (1), Yellow-Bellied, Slave Orcs are not Vicious

Gargoyles * — Infantry

Unit Size	Sp	Me	Ra	De	Att	Ne	Pts
Troop (10)	10	4+	–	3+	8	9/11	80

Special

Base Size: 25x25mm, Fly, Regeneration (3+)

Lesser Obsidian Golems — Large Infantry

Unit Size	Sp	Me	Ra	De	Att	Ne	Pts
Regiment (3)	5	4+	–	6+	9	–/14	135
Horde (6)	5	4+	–	6+	18	–/17	210

Special

Base Size: 50x50mm, Height 3, Crushing Strength (2), Shambling

Greater Obsidian Golem — Monster

Unit Size	Sp	Me	Ra	De	Att	Ne	Pts
1	5	4+	–	6+	8	–/18	160

Special

Crushing Strength (3), Shambling

Abyssal Halfbreeds — Cavalry

Unit Size	Sp	Me	Ra	De	Att	Ne	Pts
Troop (5)	8	3+	–	4+	8	11/13	125
Regiment (10)	8	3+	–	4+	16	14/16	195

Special

Crushing Strength (1), Regeneration (5+), Thunderous Charge (1)

Abyssal Grotesques — Large Cavalry

Unit Size	Sp	Me	Ra	De	Att	Ne	Pts
Regiment (3)	7	4+	–	5+	9	12/14	165
Horde (6)	7	4+	–	5+	18	16/18	250

Special

Brutal, Crushing Strength (2), Regeneration (5+), Thunderous Charge (1)

G'rog Mortar — War Engine

Unit Size	Sp	Me	Ra	De	Att	Ne	Pts
1	4	–	5+	5+	1	10/12	100

Special

Blast (D6+2), Indirect Fire, Piercing (2), Reload!

'Dragon' Fire-team — War Engine

Unit Size	Sp	Me	Ra	De	Att	Ne	Pts
1	4	–	–	4+	10	10/12	50

Special

Base Size: 25x50mm, Breath Attack (Att), Individual

Katsuchan Rocket Launcher — War Engine

Unit Size	Sp	Me	Ra	De	Att	Ne	Pts
1	4	–	5+	5+	3	10/12	85

Special

Blast (D3), Indirect Fire, Piercing (1), Reload!

Angkor Heavy Mortar — War Engine

Unit Size	Sp	Me	Ra	De	Att	Ne	Pts
1	4	–	5+	5+	1	10/12	120

Special

Blast (D6+4), Indirect Fire, Piercing (3), Reload!

Overmaster — Hero (Inf)

Unit Size	Sp	Me	Ra	De	Att	Ne	Pts
1	4	3+	–	6+	5	13/15	120

Special

Crushing Strength (1), Individual, Inspiring

Overmaster on
Great Abyssal Dragon   Hero (Mon)

Unit Size	Sp	Me	Ra	De	Att	Ne	Pts
1	10	3+	–	5+	8	17/19	280

Special

Breath Attack (10), Crushing Strength (3) Fly, Inspiring

Slavedriver   Hero (Inf)

Unit Size	Sp	Me	Ra	De	Att	Ne	Pts
1	4	5+	–	5+	1	10/12	50

Special

Individual, Inspiring

Abyssal
Halfbreed Champion   Hero (Cav)

Unit Size	Sp	Me	Ra	De	Att	Ne	Pts
1	8	3+	–	5+	6	12/14	160

Special

Crushing Strength (3), Individual, Inspiring,
Regeneration (5+)

Abyssal
Grotesque Champion   Hero (Lrg Cav)

Unit Size	Sp	Me	Ra	De	Att	Ne	Pts
1	7	3+	–	5+	5	12/14	140

Special

Brutal, Crushing Strength (2), Nimble, Regeneration
(5+), Thunderous Charge (1)

Iron-caster   Hero (Inf)

Unit Size	Sp	Me	Ra	De	Att	Ne	Pts
1	4	4+	–	5+	2	11/13	105

Special

Crushing Strength (1), Fireball (6), Heal (3 – works
only on War Engines, Golems and Immortal Guard),
Individual, Inspiring (War Engines only)

Options

• Lightning Bolt (3) for +20 pts

• Surge (8) for +15 pts

Supreme Iron-caster on Great Winged Halfbreed
Hero (Mon)

Unit Size	Sp	Me	Ra	De	Att	Ne	Pts
1	10	4+	–	5+	5	15/17	190

Special

Crushing Strength (2), Fireball (10), Fly,
Heal (4 – works only on War Engines, Golems and
Immortal Guard), Inspiring

Options

- Lightning Bolt (3) for +20 pts
- Surge (10) for +20 pts

Ba'su'su the Vile [1]
Hero (Inf)

Unit Size	Sp	Me	Ra	De	Att	Ne	Pts
1	10	3+	–	5+	8	15/17	220

Special

Base Size: 25x25mm, Crushing Strength (2),
Fly, Individual, Inspiring (Gargoyles only),
Regeneration (5+)

Vile Spawn

If your army includes Ba'su'su, for +20 pts you may
upgrade a single unit of Gargoyles to represent his
flock of elder Gargoyles. This unit has Defence 4+ and
Crushing Strength (1).

Brakki Barka [1]
Hero (Cav)

Unit Size	Sp	Me	Ra	De	At	Ne	Pts
1	8	3+	–	5+	6	14/16	200

Special

Bhardoom!, Crushing Strength (3), Individual,
Regeneration (5+)

Bhardoom!

Because of his awesome battle-cry, and what that
means to his own troops, Brakki Barka is Extremely
Inspiring (this is the same as the Inspiring special
rule, except that it has a range of 12").

GOBLIN ARMIES

Goblin Army Special Rules

Alignment: Evil

Utterly Spineless
All units in this list have the Yellow Bellied special rule, unless specified otherwise.

Sharpsticks · Infantry

Unit Size	Sp	Me	Ra	De	Att	Ne	Pts
Regiment (20)	5	5+	–	4+	15	12/14	95
Horde (40)	5	5+	–	4+	30	19/21	155
Legion (60)	5	5+	–	4+	35	25/27	230

Special
Phalanx

Rabble · Infantry

Unit Size	Sp	Me	Ra	De	Att	Ne	Pts
Regiment (20)	5	5+	–	4+	12	12/14	75
Horde (40)	5	5+	–	4+	25	19/21	125
Legion (60)	5	5+	–	4+	30	25/27	180

Spitters · Infantry

Unit Size	Sp	Me	Ra	De	Att	Ne	Pts
Regiment (20)	5	6+	5+	3+	10	12/14	85
Horde (40)	5	6+	5+	3+	20	19/21	140

Special
Bows

Mawbeasts Pack * · Cavalry

Unit Size	Sp	Me	Ra	De	Att	Ne	Pts
Troop (5)	6	3+	–	3+	6	9/11	60
Regiment (10)	6	3+	–	3+	12	12/14	95

Special
Height 1, Crushing Strength (1), Nimble, Vicious
Note that handlers models are purely decorative.

Fleabag Riders · Cavalry

Unit Size	Sp	Me	Ra	De	Att	Ne	Pts
Troop (5)	10	4+	–	4+	7	9/11	95
Regiment (10)	10	4+	–	4+	14	12/14	145
Horde (20)	10	4+	–	4+	28	17/19	255

Special
Thunderous Charge (1), Nimble

Fleabag Chariots · Large Cavalry

Unit Size	Sp	Me	Ra	De	Att	Ne	Pts
Regiment (3)	9	4+	5+	4+	8	10/12	110
Horde (6)	9	4+	5+	4+	16	13/15	170

Special
Bows, Base Size: 50x100mm, Thunderous Charge (2)

Fleabag Rider Sniffs · Cavalry

Unit Size	Sp	Me	Ra	De	Att	Ne	Pts
Troop (5)	10	5+	5+	3+	7	9/11	95
Regiment (10)	10	5+	5+	3+	14	12/14	145

Special
Bows, Nimble

Trolls
Large Infantry

Unit Size	Sp	Me	Ra	De	Att	Ne	Pts
Regiment (3)	6	4+	–	5+	9	11/14	125
Horde (6)	6	4+	–	5+	18	14/17	190

Special

Crushing Strength (2), Regeneration (5+)

Note that Trolls are not Yellow Bellied, as that would require too much intelligence on their part.

Sharpstick Thrower
War Engine

Unit Size	Sp	Me	Ra	De	Att	Ne	Pts
1	5	–	5+	4+	2	8/10	55

Special

Blast (D3), Piercing (2), Reload!

War-Trombone
War Engine

Unit Size	Sp	Me	Ra	De	Att	Ne	Pts
1	5	–	–	4+	12	8/10	65

Special

Breath Attack (Att), Piercing (1)

Big Rocks Thrower
War Engine

Unit Size	Sp	Me	Ra	De	Att	Ne	Pts
1	5	–	5+	4+	1	8/10	80

Special

Blast (D6+2), Indirect Fire, Piercing (3), Reload!

Mincer
Monster

Unit Size	Sp	Me	Ra	De	Att	Ne	Pts
1	5	4+	–	4+	(D6+6)*	9/11	80

Special

Base Size: 50x100mm, Height 3, Big Shield, Brutal, Thunderous Charge (3),

* Roll for the number of Attacks every time you resolve a melee.

Giant
Monster

Unit Size	Sp	Me	Ra	De	Att	Ne	Pts
1	7	4+	–	5+	(D6+6)*	17/19	190

Special

Brutal, Crushing Strength (3), Fury, Strider.

Note that Giants are not Yellow Bellied, as that would require too much intelligence on their part.

* Roll for the number of Attacks every time you resolve a melee.

Slasher
Monster

Unit Size	Sp	Me	Ra	De	Att	Ne	Pts
1	7	4+	–	5+	8	14/16	165

Special

Crushing Strength (2), Thunderous Charge (1)

Note that Slashers are not Yellow Bellied.

Options
• Mount a small sharpstick thrower on it – Range 36", Ra 5+, 2 ranged attacks, Piercing (2) – for +10 pts.

King
Hero (Inf)

Unit Size	Sp	Me	Ra	De	Att	Ne	Pts
1	5	4+	4+	4+	5	11/13	90

Special

Bow, Individual, Inspiring

Options
• Mount on a Fleabag, increasing Speed to 10 (+20 pts) and changing to Hero (Cav)

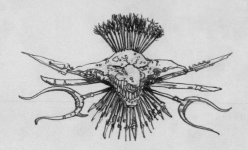

Wiz Hero (Inf)

Unit Size	Sp	Me	Ra	De	Att	Ne	Pts
1	5	5+	–	4+	1	9/11	45

Special

Individual, Lightning Bolt (3)

Options

- Wind Blast (5) for +15pts
- Bane-chant (2) for +15pts
- Fireball (6) for +15pts
- Mount on a Fleabag, increasing Speed to 10 (+15 pts) and changing to Hero (Cav)

King on Chariot Hero (Lrg Cav)

Unit Size	Sp	Me	Ra	De	Att	Ne	Pts
1	9	4+	4+	5+	7	13/15	130

Special

Bow, Base Size: 50x100mm, Inspiring, Thunderous Charge (2)

Troll Bruiser Hero (Lrg Inf)

Unit Size	Sp	Me	Ra	De	Att	Ne	Pts
1	6	3+	–	5+	5	12/15	125

Special

Crushing Strength (3), Inspiring (Trolls only), Nimble, Regeneration (5+)

Note that Trolls are not *Yellow Bellied*.

Flaggit Hero (Inf)

Unit Size	Sp	Me	Ra	De	Att	Ne	Pts
1	5	6+	–	4+	1	8/10	40

Special

Individual, Inspiring

Options

- Mount on a Fleabag, increasing Speed to 10 (+15 pts) and changing to Hero (Cav)

Magwa & Jo'os [1] Hero (Lrg Cav)

Unit Size	Sp	Me	Ra	De	Att	Ne	Pts
1	6	3+	–	4+	4	12/14	110

Special

Both models should be mounted together on a 50x50mm base, Height 1, Crushing Strength (2), Individual, Inspiring, Lightning Bolt (4), Vicious

Note that the Yellow Bellied rule in this case represents Magwa's troubles controlling his ferocious pet!

The Magwa'ns

If your army includes Magwa and Jo'os, a single Mawbeast Pack in the army is no longer Irregular – they are the Magwa'ns, a group of enthusiastic, would-be successors to the role of Jo'os handler if (when) Jo'os is finally going to devour Magwa.

Biggit Hero (Inf)

Unit Size	Sp	Me	Ra	De	Att	Ne	Pts
1	5	4+	4+	4+	3	9/11	60

Special

Bow, Individual, Inspiring

Options

- Mount on a Fleabag, increasing Speed to 10 (+15 pts) and changing to Hero (Cav)

ORC ARMIES

Orc Army Special Rules

Alignment: Evil

Tribal Might
All units in this list have Crushing Strength (1), unless specified otherwise.

Also, all infantry models in this list are on 25x25mm bases, unless specified otherwise.

Goblin Stabby Sneak
Goblin Stabby Sneaks are tiny treacherous assassins of uncommon bravado.

This unit has +1 attack.

Goblin Zappy Sneak
Zappy Sneaks are clever little imps gifted with nasty and unpredictable magical powers.

This unit has the Lightning Bolt (2) spell.

Ax   Infantry

Unit Size	Sp	Me	Ra	De	Att	Ne	Pts
Troop (10)	5	4+	–	5+	10	9/11	90
Regiment (20)	5	4+	–	5+	12	13/15	125
Horde (40)	5	4+	–	5+	25	20/22	205

Morax   Infantry

Unit Size	Sp	Me	Ra	De	Att	Ne	Pts
Troop (10)	5	3+	–	4+	20	10/12	140
Regiment (20)	5	3+	–	4+	25	14/16	200

Greatax   Infantry

Unit Size	Sp	Me	Ra	De	Att	Ne	Pts
Troop (10)	5	3+	–	4+	10	10/12	100
Regiment (20)	5	3+	–	4+	12	14/16	145
Horde (40)	5	3+	–	4+	25	21/23	240

Special
Crushing Strength (2)

Gore Riders   Cavalry

Unit Size	Sp	Me	Ra	De	Att	Ne	Pts
Troop (5)	8	3+	–	5+	8	10/12	120
Regiment (10)	8	3+	–	5+	16	13/15	185

Special
Thunderous Charge (1)

Gore Chariots   Large Cavalry

Unit Size	Sp	Me	Ra	De	Att	Ne	Pts
Regiment (3)	7	3+	–	5+	9	11/13	140
Horde (6)	7	3+	–	5+	18	14/16	215

Special
Base Size: 50x100mm, Thunderous Charge (2)

Skulks   Infantry

Unit Size	Sp	Me	Ra	De	Att	Ne	Pts
Troop (10)	6	5+	5+	3+	8	9/11	75

Special
Bows, Vanguard

Orclings *   Large Infantry

Unit Size	Sp	Me	Ra	De	Att	Ne	Pts
Regiment (3)	5	5+	–	3+	12	10/12	60
Horde (6)	5	5+	–	3+	24	13/15	90

Special
Height 0, Vicious,
Orclings do not have Crushing Strength

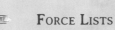

Trolls *
Large Infantry

Unit Size	Sp	Me	Ra	De	Att	Ne	Pts
Regiment (3)	6	4+	–	5+	9	11/14	125
Horde (6)	6	4+	–	5+	18	14/17	190

Special

Crushing Strength (2), Regeneration (5+)

Fight Wagons
Large Cavalry

Unit Size	Sp	Me	Ra	De	Att	Ne	Pts
Regiment (3)	7	3+	–	5+	15	11/13	170
Horde (6)	7	3+	–	5+	30	14/16	260

Special

Base Size: 50x100mm

War Drum
Monster

Unit Size	Sp	Me	Ra	De	Att	Ne	Pts
1	5	4+	–	4+	3	-/11	80

Special

Height 1, Great Thunder

Great Thunder

While within 6" of one or more war drums, friendly non-allied units have +2 to their waver and rout nerve values. War Drums themselves are not affected by this rule.

Giant
Monster

Unit Size	Sp	Me	Ra	De	Att	Ne	Pts
1	7	4+	–	5+	D6+6*	17/19	190

Special

Brutal, Crushing Strength (3), Fury, Strider

* Roll for the number of Attacks every time you resolve a melee.

Krudger
Hero (Inf)

Unit Size	Sp	Me	Ra	De	Att	Ne	Pts
1	5	3+	–	5+	5	12/14	130

Special

Crushing Strength (2), Individual, Inspiring

Options

- Mount on a Gore, increasing Speed to 8 (+20 pts) and changing to Hero (Cav)
- Goblin Stabby Sneak (+15 pts)
- Goblin Zappy Sneak (+15 pts)

Krudger on Slasher
Hero (Mon)

Unit Size	Sp	Me	Ra	De	Att	Ne	Pts
1	7	3+	–	5+	10	16/18	235

Special

Crushing Strength (3), Inspiring

Options

- Mount on a Winged Slasher instead, increasing Speed to 10 and gaining the Fly special rule (+50 pts)

Krudger on Gore Chariot
Hero (Lrg Cav)

Unit Size	Sp	Me	Ra	De	Att	Ne	Pts
1	7	3+	–	5+	7	14/16	185

Special
Base Size: 50x100mm, Crushing Strength (2), Inspiring, Thunderous Charge (2)

Options
• Goblin Stabby Sneak (+15 pts)
• Goblin Zappy Sneak (+15 pts)

Flagger
Hero (Inf)

Unit Size	Sp	Me	Ra	De	Att	Ne	Pts
1	5	4+	–	4+	1	9/11	50

Special
Individual, Inspiring

Options
• Mount on a Gore, increasing Speed to 8 (+15 pts) and changing to Hero (Cav)

Godspeaker
Hero (Inf)

Unit Size	Sp	Me	Ra	De	Att	Ne	Pts
1	5	3+	–	4+	2	10/12	75

Special
Fireball (9), Individual,

For every friendly non-allied Horde within 6", increase the amount of dice rolled for all spells by 1.

Options
• Bane Chant (2) for +15pts
• Heal (2) for +10pts
• Mount on a Gore, increasing Speed to 8 (+15 pts) and changing to Hero (Cav)

Troll Bruiser
Hero (Large Inf)

Unit Size	Sp	Me	Ra	De	Att	Ne	Pts
1	6	3+	–	5+	5	12/15	125

Special
Crushing Strength (3), Inspiring (Trolls only), Nimble, Regeneration (5+)

Gakamak [1]
Hero (Inf)

Unit Size	Sp	Me	Ra	De	At	Ne	Pts
1	5	2+	–	5+	7	13/15	210

Special
Crushing Strength (3), Individual, Very Inspiring, Vicious

Options
• Mount on a Gore, increasing Speed to 8 (+30 pts)

Wip the Half-cast [1]
Hero (Inf)

Unit Size	Sp	Me	Ra	De	Att	Ne	Pts
1	6	4+	–	4+	1	11/13	90

Special
Elite, Heal (3), Individual, Inspiring (Orclings only), Lightning Bolt (3)

Note: Wip does not have Crushing Strength

Wip's Playmates
If your army includes Wip, for +5 points you may upgrade a single unit of Orclings to represent Wip's affectionate playmates and adorers. This unit has the Headstrong special rule.

UNDEAD ARMIES

Undead Army Special Rules

Alignment: Evil

Evil Dead

All units in this list have Lifeleech (1) unless specified otherwise.

Undead Giant Rats (or are they Dogs?)

These creatures follow the shambling hordes into battle, their venomous bites helping to spread the curse of the living death.

The unit increases its Lifeleech (1) to Lifeleech (2).

Skeleton Warriors   Infantry

Unit Size	Sp	Me	Ra	De	Att	Ne	Pts
Troop (10)	5	5+	–	4+	10	–/12	65
Regiment (20)	5	5+	–	4+	12	–/16	90
Horde (40)	5	5+	–	4+	25	–/23	150

Special
Shambling

Options
• Undead Giant Rats (Dogs?) (+10 pts)

Skeleton Spearmen   Infantry

Unit Size	Sp	Me	Ra	De	Att	Ne	Pts
Troop (10)	5	5+	–	4+	10	–/12	75
Regiment (20)	5	5+	–	4+	15	–/16	105
Horde (40)	5	5+	–	4+	30	–/23	175

Special
Phalanx, Shambling

Options
• Undead Giant Rats (Dogs?) (+10 pts)

Skeleton Archers   Infantry

Unit Size	Sp	Me	Ra	De	Att	Ne	Pts
Troop (10)	5	6+	5+	3+	8	–/12	75
Regiment (20)	5	6+	5+	3+	10	–/16	100
Horde (40)	5	6+	5+	3+	20	–/23	165

Special
Bows, Shambling

Options
• Undead Giant Rats (Dogs?) (+10 pts)

Ghouls   Infantry

Unit Size	Sp	Me	Ra	De	Att	Ne	Pts
Troop (10)	6	4+	–	3+	10	8/10	65
Regiment (20)	6	4+	–	3+	12	12/14	90
Horde (40)	6	4+	–	3+	25	19/21	150

Soul Reaver Infantry — Infantry

Unit Size	Sp	Me	Ra	De	Att	Ne	Pts
Troop (10)	6	3+	–	5+	20	11/13	180
Regiment (20)	6	3+	–	5+	25	15/17	260

Special
Crushing Strength (2), Lifeleech (2)

Revenants — Infantry

Unit Size	Sp	Me	Ra	De	Att	Ne	Pts
Troop (10)	5	4+	–	5+	10	–/13	85
Regiment (20)	5	4+	–	5+	12	–/17	120
Horde (40)	5	4+	–	5+	25	–/24	200

Special
Shambling

Options
• Exchange shields for two-handed weapons for free
  (lower Defence to 4+, gain Crushing Strength (1))
• Undead Giant Rats (Dogs?) (+10 pts)

Soul Reaver Cavalry — Cavalry

Unit Size	Sp	Me	Ra	De	Att	Ne	Pts
Troop (5)	8	3+	–	6+	10	12/14	195
Regiment (10)	8	3+	–	6+	20	15/17	300

Special
Crushing Strength (1), Lifeleech (2),
Thunderous Charge (2)

Revenant Cavalry — Cavalry

Unit Size	Sp	Me	Ra	De	Att	Ne	Pts
Troop (5)	8	4+	–	5+	8	–/14	110
Regiment (10)	8	4+	–	5+	16	–/17	170

Special
Shambling, Thunderous Charge (2)

Wraiths — Infantry

Unit Size	Sp	Me	Ra	De	Att	Ne	Pts
Troop (10)	10	4+	–	6+	10	–/12	140
Regiment (20)	10	4+	–	6+	12	–/16	200

Special
Crushing Strength (1), Fly, Shambling

Mummies — Infantry

Unit Size	Sp	Me	Ra	De	Att	Ne	Pts
Troop (10)	5	4+	–	5+	10	–/14	120
Regiment (20)	5	4+	–	5+	12	–/18	170

Special
Crushing Strength (2), Regeneration (5+), Shambling

Zombies — Infantry

Unit Size	Sp	Me	Ra	De	Att	Ne	Pts
Regiment (20)	5	5+	–	3+	15	–/15	80
Horde (40)	5	5+	–	3+	30	–/22	130
Legion (60)	5	5+	–	3+	40	–/28	190

Special
Shambling

Options
• Undead Giant Rats (Dogs?) (+10 pts)

Zombie Trolls — Large Infantry

Unit Size	Sp	Me	Ra	De	Att	Ne	Pts
Regiment (3)	6	4+	–	4+	9	–/15	115
Horde (6)	6	4+	–	4+	18	–/18	175

Special
Crushing Strength (2), Shambling.

Werewolves — Large Infantry

Unit Size	Sp	Me	Ra	De	Att	Ne	Pts
Regiment (3)	9	3+	–	5+	9	12/14	160
Horde (6)	9	3+	–	5+	18	15/17	245

Special
Crushing Strength (1), Nimble

Wights — Large Infantry

Unit Size	Sp	Me	Ra	De	Att	Ne	Pts
Regiment (3)	6	4+	–	5+	9	–/14	155
Horde (6)	6	4+	–	5+	18	–/17	235

Special
Brutal, Crushing Strength (3), Shambling

Balefire Catapult — War Engine

Unit Size	Sp	Me	Ra	De	Att	Ne	Pts
1	5	–	5+	4+	1	–/11	100

Special

Blast (D6+2), Indirect Fire, Piercing (2), *Reload!,* Shambling, Vicious

Revenant King — Hero (Inf)

Unit Size	Sp	Me	Ra	De	Att	Ne	Pts
1	5	4+	–	5+	5	14/16	120

Special

Crushing Strength (1), Individual, Inspiring, Surge (6)

Options

- Mount on an undead horse, increasing Speed to 8 (+20 pts) and changing to Hero (Cav)

Revenant King on Undead Wyrm — Hero (Mon)

Unit Size	Sp	Me	Ra	De	Att	Ne	Pts
1	7	4+	–	5+	9	18/20	190

Special

Crushing Strength (3), Surge (6), Inspiring

Options

- Mount on a Winged Wyrm, increasing Speed to 10 and gaining Fly (+45 pts).

Undead Army Standard Bearer — Hero (Inf)

Unit Size	Sp	Me	Ra	De	Att	Ne	Pts
1	5	5+	–	4+	1	–/13	50

Special

Individual, Inspiring, Shambling

Options

- Mount on an undead horse, increasing Speed to 8 (+15 pts) and changing to Hero (Cav)

Cursed Pharaoh — Hero (Inf)

Unit Size	Sp	Me	Ra	De	Att	Ne	Pts
1	5	3+	–	6+	5	15/17	145

Special

Crushing Strength (2), Individual, Inspiring, Regeneration (5+), Surge (6)

Vampire Lord — Hero (Inf)

Unit Size	Sp	Me	Ra	De	Att	Ne	Pts
1	7	3+	–	6+	8	14/16	220

Special

Crushing Strength (2), Individual, Inspiring, Lifeleech (2), Surge (3)

Options

- Heal (2) for +10pts
- Lightning Bolt (3) for +20pts
- Mount on an undead horse, increasing Speed to 9 (+15 pts) and changing to Hero (Cav)

Vampire on Undead Pegasus — Hero (Lrg Cav)

Unit Size	Sp	Me	Ra	De	Att	Ne	Pts
1	10	3+	–	5+	8	14/16	245

Special

Crushing Strength (2), Fly, Inspiring, Lifeleech (2), Surge (3)

Options

- Heal (2) for +10pts
- Lightning Bolt (3) for +20pts

Vampire on Undead Dragon — Hero (Mon)

Unit Size	Sp	Me	Ra	De	Att	Ne	Pts
1	10	3+	–	5+	10	17/19	330

Special

Breath Attack (10), Crushing Strength (3), Fly, Inspiring, Lifeleech (2), Surge (3)

Options

- Heal (2) for +10pts
- Lightning Bolt (3) for +20pts

Liche King
Hero (Inf)

Unit Size	Sp	Me	Ra	De	Att	Ne	Pts
1	5	5+	–	4+	1	14/16	145

Special
Individual, Inspiring, Regeneration (5+), Surge (12)

Options
• Heal (6) for +20pts, or free to replace Surge.
• Lightning Bolt (5) for +35pts
• Bane-chant (3) for +20pts
• Mount on an undead horse, increasing Speed to 8 (+20 pts) and changing to Hero (Cav)

Necromancer
Hero (Inf)

Unit Size	Sp	Me	Ra	De	Att	Ne	Pts
1	5	5+	–	4+	1	10/12	85

Special
Individual, Surge (8)

Options
• Heal (3) for +15pts, or free to replace Surge.
• Lightning Bolt (3) for +20pts
• Bane-chant (2) for +15pts
• Mount on an undead horse, increasing Speed to 8 (+15 pts) and changing to Hero (Cav)

Lykanis
Hero (Lrg Inf)

Unit Size	Sp	Me	Ra	De	Att	Ne	Pts
1	9	3+	–	5+	5	13/15	145

Special
Crushing Strength (2), Inspiring (Werewolves only), Nimble

Lady Ilona [1]
Hero (Inf)

Unit Size	Sp	Me	Ra	De	At	Ne	Pts
1	8	3+	–	6+	8	14/16	280

Special
Crushing Strength (3), Heal (3), Individual, Inspiring, Lifeleech (2), Lightning Bolt (3), Surge (3)

The Promise of Love Eternal
Enemy Heroes attacking Lady Ilona receive –1 to hit in melee.

Mhorgoth the Faceless [1]
Hero (Inf)

Unit Size	Sp	Me	Ra	De	Att	Ne	Pts
1	10	4+	–	6+	1	17/19	270

Special
Bane-chant (4), Fireball (15), Fly, Heal (6), Individual, Lightning Bolt (6), Regeneration (5+), Surge (12), Very Inspiring

Touch of Darkness
If your army includes Mhorgoth, you may upgrade any one non-allied unit in the army (except for Heroes), imbuing it with the arcane power of the Faceless himself (+25 points). The unit thus upgraded has the Regeneration (5+) special rule.